HOW TO DELIVER TRAINING

For Jacky
special friend and major influence
on both my life and views of learning.

True friendship is never serene
- Marie de Rabutin-Chantal

HOW TO DELIVER TRAINING

Martin Orridge

Gower

Published by
Gower Publishing Limited
Gower House
Croft Road
Aldershot
Hampshire GU11 3HR
England

Gower
Old Post Road
Brookfield
Vermont 05036
USA

Martin Orridge has asserted his right under the Copyright, Designs and Patents Act 1988 to be identified as the author of this work.

British Library Cataloguing in Publication Data
Orridge, Martin, 1947–
  How to deliver training
  1. Employees – Training of – Handbooks, manuals, etc.
  I. Title
  658.3'12404

  ISBN 0 566 07913 5

Library of Congress Cataloging-in-Publication Data
Orridge, Martin, 1947–
  How to deliver training /Martin Orridge
    p. cm.
  Includes bibliographical references and index.
  ISBN 0–566–07913–5 (hardback)
  1. Employees—Training of— Study and teaching.
  I. Title
  HF5549.5.T7078 1998   97–31502
  658.3'12404—dc21   CIP

Typeset in 10 point Plantin Light by Photoprint, Torquay, Devon, and printed in Great Britain by MPG Books Limited, Bodmin.

CONTENTS

LIST OF FIGURES AND TABLES

Figures

Tables

PREFACE

There are only two ways to live your life. One is as though nothing is a miracle. The other is as though everything is a miracle.

Albert Einstein

I can think of few activities more rewarding than helping someone learn. Our continual desire and enthusiasm for knowledge never cease to amaze me. I enjoy seeing people's creative potential unlocked and watching fresh and new ideas tumble out. I get a kick from observing people mastering a new skill and always feel a mixture of happiness and humility when someone shakes my hand to thank me at the end of a training event. People development is a challenging and exciting role, one that I have enjoyed for many years. We have a great responsibility, which is why I like to remember the words from Supertramp's Logical Song:

> When I was young, it seemed that life was so
> wonderful, a miracle, it was beautiful,
> magical . . .
> But then they sent me away to teach me how to
> be sensible, logical, responsible, practical . . .
> Then they showed me a world where I could be
> dependable, clinical, cynical. . . .

> – We must keep training wonderful and magical.

The aim of this book is to provide a practical guide to delivering successful developmental events to both managers wishing to run 'in team' exercises and those entering the training profession. The book comprises four sections. The Introduction expands on the need for training and trainers and is followed by Part I, 'Designing a Successful Training Event' and Part II, 'Running a Successful Training Event'. These are based on what I have discovered over the years whilst I have planned, organized and delivered events as both a manager and trainer. The book includes many anecdotal 'cameos' or stories. I have found that the 'theory' is often more easily remembered as a result of accessing the story. To help with the learning process I have also included a few interactive exercises. At the end of the text is a compendium of documents and forms that might be useful during the training cycle.

In short this book is a collection of ideas, tips, tools, checklists and techniques plus a little theory that anyone can dip into to help them run a successful event.

I hope I have illustrated my enthusiasm for the role and I would like to thank my children, Robert and Jenny, and my many colleagues and friends for their encouragement whilst the book has been in preparation.

Martin Orridge
Atticus Ltd
Century House
74 Bounty Road
Basingstoke
Hants, RG21 3BZ

INTRODUCTION

You cannot teach a man anything, you can only help him to find it for himself.
Galileo Galilei

Training and development are vital to successful business. One has only to
look at our everyday business language, with words like downsizing,
rightsizing, re-engineering etc. becoming common place, to reflect the
apparent need for continual reorganization. Yet, as many readers may
recognize, this is not a new phenomenon. Even in ancient times there
seemed to be a need for constant organizational change. Petronius Arbiter,
the Roman philosopher, observed: 'I was to learn in later life that we tend
to meet any new situation by re-organizing; and a wonderful method it
can be for creating the illusion of progress while producing confusion,
inefficiency and demoralisation.'

Two thousand years later the same appears to be true. In the drive to
maintain competitive advantage management constantly strives to
introduce new ways of doing business. In order to reduce the Petronius
effect management must ensure that staff acquire only those fresh skills
and knowledge that are in line with the new business imperatives. Change
demands training! Consequently, the organization's Personnel, People
Development or Training functions are in a unique position. Not only
must they find new and original ways of developing staff, but they are also
a key element of the change process itself. However, the Personnel and
Training functions are today not seen as the sole providers of people
development. There is more emphasis on self-development and managers
frequently take a leadership role in training and developing their people,
both with and without the involvement of the Training department.

Why bother to train?

Training is often seen as the icing on the company cake: it can be spread
very thinly or even dispensed with altogether when times are tough. There
are a number of reasons commonly given for not undertaking training:

- So many people in the job market – place the right advertisement and with careful selection you will recruit just the person you need without having to train them.
- It is a long-term investment – business is short term and so are investments.
- Money can be better spent elsewhere – training comes somewhere below redecorating the office toilets.
- It is not seen as mainstream to the organization – not part of the above mentioned metaphoric cake, but a useful addition when times are good.

If this is the case, then why should we train? Following on from the Introduction, training is required because:

- of the changing environment of organizations. Continual change is a fact of business life and responding appropriately is often the key to survival. Consequently people's jobs, and how they do them, are also liable to change. Successful organizations will help their people to meet the challenges of change.
- of the needs of business. Staff need to combine skill, knowledge and experience to match the role they are required to undertake. Successful organizations will align training to business needs.
- ignorance is not bliss. It can be very expensive. Lack of trained staff can result in mistakes being made, waste, low motivation, high labour turnover and unhappy suppliers and customers. Successful organizations ensure, by a variety of training approaches, that staff are kept up to date with the requirements of the job.

Recognizing the importance of training as part of a healthy and vibrant organization is but the first step. The second step is to identify the individual needs of the organization and then to relate them to the training requirements.

What is training?

When I first became involved in people development a colleague succinctly explained to me the difference between education and training. She said she was very happy for her thirteen-year-old daughter to have sex education but would never agree to sex training. Education is concerned with the transfer of information or knowledge whilst training should not only impart knowledge but also develop skills and change attitudes. Successful training in the organization requires a learning process in which the learning opportunities are structured by both management and training staff. The objective is to develop the skills, knowledge, experience and attitudes of the employees so that they achieve effective work performance which is consistent with the organization's aims or goals. To be successful:

- training should be a means to an end not an end in itself; it must be an integral part of the organization
- job performance specifications must be defined and should cover the full range of business processes
- management must be responsible for ensuring that staff are effectively trained
- development should take place at all levels in the organization, from the most junior to the most senior – training does not stop once you become a board member
- training must be a collaboration between management, employees, training and personnel staffs
- managers and trainers must understand how people learn
- training must be integrated into the work processes with a systematic approach to identifying training needs.

What does a trainer do?

The trainer's role is to help facilitate the acquisition of knowledge, development of skills and the change of attitudes that will enable a person to be effective in their role. Like all other members of staff the trainer must possess the appropriate knowledge, skills and attitude to be effective in developing people. The remainder of this book is dedicated to assist anybody undertaking this challenging role.

PART *1*

DESIGNING A SUCCESSFUL TRAINING EVENT

Drawn by Simon Jarvis

Tell me and I'll forget. Show me and I may not remember. Involve me and I'll understand.

Native American Proverb

There are many elements in the design of a successful training event. The first step is to identify your needs. Armed with this identification and some knowledge of how people learn you should be able to design an event which, by using appropriate training, meets the organization's needs. A good design, however, is not enough to ensure successful training. You also need to consider the skill, knowledge and experience of the trainer(s) who will run the event and the roles and responsibilities of the trainee and their manager. The attitudes and actions of trainee and their manager are critical to a successful outcome, because attendance at a training event is unlikely to fulfil all the development needs. The training course is only one element. What happens before and after the event are just as, if not more, important.

The four chapters in Part I examine the above elements in more detail. By following these approaches you can put into place the running of a successful training event even before the first delegate arrives.

1 IDENTIFYING PEOPLE DEVELOPMENT NEEDS

Life is a succession of lessons, which must be lived to be understood.
Ralph Waldo Emerson

Whilst the prime focus of this book is training course design and delivery it is worth taking a small step backwards to see how training fits into the people development process. The reasons are twofold. Firstly you can better understand a system by viewing it from the outside and, secondly, a brief exploration of some alternative methods of people development will help to set the whole process in context.

There are two approaches to people development, the corporate approach and the individual one. In an ideal world these would partner each other exactly with all individual development being a subset of the corporate plan. At best, attempts are made to link the two. At worst, individual training is requested and delivered with scant regard for business requirements, which is often the case where training is seen as a person's right.

An organization's training needs can arise in many ways.

- They may be driven by the organization's change of strategic direction and form an important part of the change initiative. Whether the organization is a leader or follower in its chosen market will determine whether training forms a part of the strategic planning process or merely reacts to sudden environmental changes.
- Individual, team or company performance may be poor when standards or goals are not achieved.
- Mistakes may be made which affect organizational performance or even health or safety issues.
- Customer complaints, possibly resulting from any of the above, may provide useful pointers for additional training.
- Annual appraisals and performance reviews often identify training/ development needs.

- Individuals might ask for help if they feel they are not performing satisfactorily, if their job content changes or if they have taken on additional responsibilities.

Any of the above together with changes in legislation and/or procedures may result in a training needs review.

Finally, when conducting a review, always check what business added value will be achieved by undertaking the training. Resources, time and money are too valuable to waste and there may be better non-training solutions, for example job redesign, to the problem. When examining the problem remember the saying, 'Give a child a hammer and everything's a nail.' Don't make training a hammer.

Conducting a strategic review

Q. HOW DO YOU EAT AN ELEPHANT?
A. ONE SLICE AT A TIME.

The training challenge faced by most organizations today is how to integrate business and people development. Business development is typically described in terms of the products, services, processes and the technology employed to achieve identified business objectives. The objectives have in turn been derived from the business strategy. In addition to developing people to support the implementation of the business strategy, it is also necessary to develop simultaneously the systems they use to achieve best practice within the industry. If this challenge is not accepted, and 'business as usual' remains the order of the day, the consequences will range across the financial spectrum from wasted training budgets to total business failure. At first sight this may appear an immense task, yet planning training and development is essentially no different from planning any other business operation with similar problems in terms of timing, resourcing and financial constraints. When faced with this sort of problem, consider the question and answer at the beginning of this section and think of ways to carve up the 'training elephant'. For example, strategic or business development elements can be considered separately from the operational and best practice elements. Alternatively, the 'elephant' can be divided into business units or geography. This approach makes the challenge more manageable and enables different processes to be selected for the collection of training needs data. The chosen route will depend on available resources and prevailing politics.

Strategic training initiatives

The alignment of training to the business development strategy is but one piece of the business strategy jigsaw. Training is a subset of the human resources element of the total business strategy. The business strategy will also include other constituent elements, for example, information systems, logistics, product and services, R&D, etc.

Within the training part of the human resources strategy it is HR management's responsibility to:

- formulate and publish policy and plans for training
- set up the systems for identifying training needs and for ensuring their effective delivery
- provide the resources, manpower and materials.

In some years the formulation of strategic training initiatives might represent a very small aspect of total human resources work load, yet in times of great change it can become very significant.

The challenge faced by many organizations is how to develop a corporate approach which is flexible enough to respond to unexpected change whilst maintaining a strategy that integrates business and people development. To survive long term, businesses must consider the following development areas:

- developing products and services, their processes and technology, to meet corporate business objectives
- developing people and systems to increase their capabilities to support the implementation of the corporate strategy
- developing all of the above to achieve best practice, both inter and intra industry.

Consequently programmes need to be developed that take account of:

- all the organization's employees
- the full career span of all employees
- the full range of business and management processes
- all products and services including the current range and prioritized future developments.

An integrated business and people development plan combines all of these elements and is developed from both the business strategy and objectives together with information on best practices.

This integrated approach will in turn drive the people development strategy.

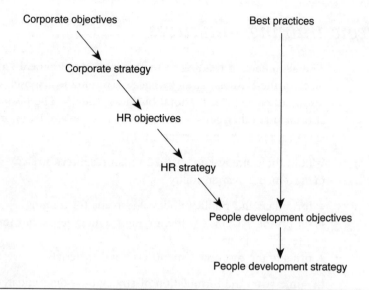

Figure 1.1 An integrated business and people development plan

The HR objective is just one set of objectives driven by the corporate strategy. Other examples are IT objectives, product and services objectives, real estate objectives. Whilst a cascade (see Figure 1.1) demonstrates the logical flow there are also many linkages and dependencies between the various sets, particularly with the people development objectives. It is a key role of senior management to maintain a balanced approach. For example, a general may have been sent twice as many pistols as he needs but no ammunition. His effectiveness has been seriously curtailed. In the same way a business can be severely damaged by failing to balance all the elements.

Strategic training initiative process

HR introduces a strategic training initiative when the organization announces a radical plan to maintain or achieve competitive advantage. In such situations it is unlikely that minor modifications to existing people development programmes will suffice.

The STI process is based on John F. Rockart's* work on critical success factors (CSFs). He defines them as: 'The key areas of the business in which high performance is essential if objectives and goals are to be met'.

---

* John F. Rockart, 'Chief executives define their own data needs', *Harvard Business Review*, 1979.

CSFs are driven by the business objectives, which are in turn driven by the mission. They form a hierarchy as shown in Figure 1.2.

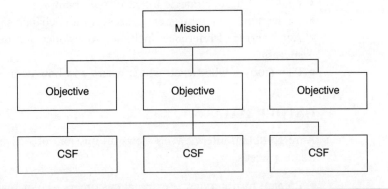

Figure 1.2 CSF hierarchy

People development and training contribute greatly to an organization's achievement of its mission. For example, in the Cameo on p. 11 the mission would have been 'to provide an excellent service that is recognized by our customers as second to none'. This resulted in the staffing objective: 'to have highly customer focused front line staff'. A critical success factor was identified as 'having a customer first attitude'.

The objectives and CSFs, or for that matter an organization's mission, are not plucked out of thin air. They should be derived from in-depth research and discussion between senior management. Once senior management has decided on the strategic direction in terms of mission, objectives and possibly some top-level CSFs it is then necessary to convert them into an actionable training and development programme (see Figure 1.3).

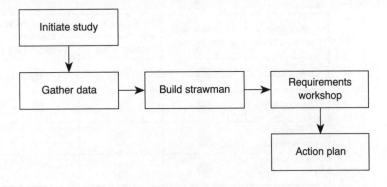

Figure 1.3 Strategic training initiative process

INITIATE STUDY

Aim: To launch a successful study.

- Understand the strategic intent of the organization.
- Understand which business processes must change significantly.
- Agree terms of reference, including milestones and definitions of success.
- Plan study – who, what, when, where and how data is to be obtained.

GATHER DATA

Aim: To obtain interviewee's views on mission, objectives and critical training needs.

- Prepare for interview – external customers, senior management, and front-line staff – using different approaches for each type of interviewee.

Determine views on mission, objective and critical training needs. Some information may be available from earlier work on business strategy and mission.

BUILD STRAWMAN

Aim: To aggregate results on interviews. A strawman is built by the consultant or project team and is the first possible solution to the training requirements for each business objective and business process.

- Write up interviews.
- Build strawman using your results in Tables 1.1 and 1.2:

Table 1.1 Business objective/Critical skill requirement

Business objective/CSR	Increase mkt. share by 10%	Increase effective use of technology	Develop better supplier relationships	Establish culture to promote change
Negotiation	●		●	
Team building	◉		◉	●
Project management	◉	◉		
Systems design	●	◉		◉

Key   Strong support ●   Partial support ◉

A critical skill requirement is a 'can do' statement, a capability for the objective or activity, e.g. work in a team. It is a combination of expertise and competency. Expertise is any specialist subject knowledge which is necessary in order to perform the activity; competency is the skills, techniques and behaviours that will maximize the impact of the specialist knowledge. Expertise can be varied, diverse and dynamic; competency is broad based and stable.

Business objectives are the goals, e.g. increase market share by 10 per cent. *Key activities* are linked together to describe the business process. For example, analyse market needs, segment the market, develop a portfolio of strategy alternatives etc. might describe the start of a develop marketing solutions process.

Table 1.2   Critical skill requirement/Business process

Critical skill requirement /Business process	Negotiation	Team building	Project management	Systems design
Sales	●	◉	◉	◉
Product development		◉	●	●
Field service	●	◉	◉	
Career planning		◉		

Key   Strong support ●   Partial support ◉

- Analyse results.
- Review.

REQUIREMENTS WORKSHOP

Aim: To identify the gaps in staff skill, knowledge and experience that will affect achievement of the organization's mission. Those attending will be drawn from the people who were interviewed for the strawman data and members of the training function.

- Present strawman.
- Discuss and obtain consensus.

OR

- Brainstorm the critical skill requirements for each objective and key activity.
- Discuss and obtain consensus.

THEN

- Map critical training needs against business objectives (see Table 1.1).
- Map critical training needs against main business processes (see Table 1.2).

ACTION PLAN

- Establish priorities (see Table 1.3).
- Identify ownership.
- Identify and agree training approaches.
- Establish milestones for course design and development.

Table 1.3 Ranking and capability table

	Current capability	Required capability	Difference
Teamworking	5 persons	100 persons	95 persons
Negotiation	0 persons	50 persons	50 persons
Systems design	50 persons	40 persons	−10 persons
....			

Capability was earlier described as a combination of expertise and competency. Therefore when designing a corporate intervention these two elements should be considered both separately and together. Various critical skill requirements may be covered simultaneously if competency development is provided to all staff. Expertise development can then be undertaken using a much more focused approach which targets individuals or small groups.

Cameo

'Slicing up the elephant'

A multinational company wished to change its strategic focus from being recognized as providing technical excellence (but little or no service) to service excellence leadership position in the market. Whilst the mission appeared to be straightforward and crystal clear, the HR implications, particularly with regard to training, were enormous. A great deal of elephant slicing was necessary to break the project down into digestible chunks. The first step was to identify the needs, in this case to talk to customers and find out what they understood by service excellence and expected from an excellent supplier.

Before any data was gathered the programme was sliced up still further so that three categories could be developed: front-line face-to-face dealings, back office support to both front-line staff and customers, and all support systems. A number of projects were initiated that identified the critical skill requirements for success in each of the categories. Each project was sliced up still further by separating the staff that worked in each, face-to-face or support. It was then possible to identify the current levels of skill, knowledge and experience within the organization and make a relatively straightforward step to identify the training needs gap across each category. This slicing approach provided for discrete and manageable assignments for the task forces. Training requirements were identified in less than three months and training programmes implemented within six. The elephant had been eaten.

Poor performance, mistakes and complaints

Poor performance is often regarded as a trigger for undertaking training needs analysis. There may well be other underlying issues, however, instead of or in addition to the provision of training.

RECOGNIZING POOR PERFORMANCE

Poor performance can manifest itself in a number of ways:

- customer complaints
- complaints from suppliers or other connected/external stakeholders
- internal arguments focusing on assigning fault or blame

- low quality
- failure to meet financial goals
- failure to meet deadlines or project milestones
- failure to achieve other internal metrics
- 'fudging' of internal metrics and/or objectives to meet performance goals/bonuses.

From a training needs analysis standpoint you have a great deal of potential data available to judge a person's or team's performance.

- Examine the job description(s) to identify the skill, knowledge and experience needed to undertake the job(s) satisfactorily.
- Consider the objectives that have been set for the individual or team.
- In which of the above areas is the individual or team not performing adequately?

If the shortfalls in performance are caused by the lack of skills, knowledge or experience then training, coaching or job rotation may be appropriate. But before taking action on improving skills, the following elements should also be considered:

- Metrics and rewards. Are they appropriate and do all the necessary tasks have incentives?
- Organizational structure. How do we divide up and control the work?
- Policies. Are company policies preventing the desired performance?
- Business processes. Do the processes support the business objectives and principles?
- Resourcing. Is a lack of people/equipment preventing the desired performance?
- Is there sufficient time?
- Relationships. Are colleagues, bosses or management style blocking the desired performance?
- Is there conflict with technology?
- Leadership. Does someone keep all the above elements in balance?

Failure to consider these other causes will often lead to only a marginal improvement in performance as a result of a training intervention. As a training manager or trainer you run the risk of being the scapegoat when performance does not improve.

Do not take a request for training at face value. When undertaking training needs analysis consider all possible causes of poor performance. If it looks as though there are some underlying issues which are outside your comfort level, involve your organizational design, or business process re-engineering colleagues (or whatever else they might be called) in the project. Better to enlarge the scope than spend your training budget ineffectively. Also, there could be further training needs associated with remedying these other elements, so you would have even more work!

Such a potentially diverse project would typically form part of a management consultancy and is beyond the scope of this book. There are many books available should you wish to explore the role of the consultant more fully. *Flawless Consulting* or *Client-Centred Consulting* (see Recommended Reading) are good places to start.

Appraisals

Appraisals typically use formal techniques for assessing individuals with a view to advising them of their progress, improving their performance and identifying potential. Many organizations have an annual appraisal scheme when the manager and the member of staff review performance during the previous year, determine a score or rating which may affect the employee's pay and identify development needs. Apart from this formal annual process, the manager should continue staff appraisal by regularly reviewing the performance of his/her staff and providing appropriate support to resolve any problems. Poor performance should be addressed immediately in ways similar to those described in the previous section. If a manager is running the team effectively there should be no surprises when the formal appraisal is conducted. Unfortunately this does not always happen and I have known cases where two to three years have passed without any staff appraisal even though there is an annual process in place. The most common reason given for not carrying out this task is that the member of staff has had many different managers during the period and none feels they know the person well enough to conduct an appraisal. This is unacceptable. Performance appraisal should be a continuous process. The manager is not doing his/her job properly.

The formal annual appraisal provides the opportunity, or even a trigger, for reflection back over the previous year and to plan for the future. Exploring the future may identify the following needs:

- to consider any performance problems (this should not be a surprise to either side)
- to provide skills for succession planning or planned departmental changes

• to provide skills for identified and agreed career move aspirations.

The last two should be part of human resources strategy. The appraisal report may contain an employee development section that triggers HR to identify the appropriate development intervention or, more likely, the manager and/or appraisee will approach HR for a development solution. The roles and responsibilities of the manager, trainer and trainee will be examined in Chapter 5.

Developing training needs

The earlier sections of this chapter indicated the various sources of training needs at both the strategic and operational levels within an organization. The need is often defined too generally to enable the rapid identification of a training solution, perhaps because of a lack of precision in the language used. Try the following exercise. (To help you to visualize the situation, you may want to close your eyes.)

1. Imagine a cube.
2. Once you have visualized the cube, cut it in half.
3. Once you have cut it in half, cut in half again.
4. Now get rid of the cube.
5. Open your eyes (if you chose to close them).

At first sight the instructions appear precise, but let us examine them in more detail.

Imagine a cube. We all know what a cube looks like; it has six equal faces, or does it? Perhaps you imaged an open line drawing. Mine was white, what colour was yours? Mine was rotating, was yours?
Cut in half, etc. I cut mine in half diagonally each time, did you? What happened to the cube? Did it fall apart?
Get rid of the cube. Mine was made of sugar and I dissolved it in some coffee to get rid of it. How did you get rid of yours?

Training needs, such as 'Improve communication skills' or 'Increase financial awareness', are often presented like the cube. But does 'Improve communication skills', for example, mean present information formally to customers, or sell decisions of others to your own staff? It could be either, both or something entirely different. It may be necessary to probe quite deeply to understand the real requirements. Job descriptions or specifications can sometimes help to identify skills that will develop the needs or the 4W cascade can provide the solution.

THE 4W CASCADE

The 4W cascade is a structured approach which is used to tease out the underlying training needs.

First level
What is the need?
Why is this training required?
When would the training be used?
Where would the training be used?
Having obtained answers to the above, move on to the second level.

Second level
What *specific* capabilities (can do's) are needed?
Why are these capabilities needed?
When would these capabilities be used?★
Where would the capabilities be used?★

The answer to the two questions indicated ★ may be the same as in the first level but a recap will ensure you have a complete understanding of the needs.

In some instances it may be necessary to refine this even further by exploring 'What skills?', 'Why these skills?', 'What techniques?', 'Why these techniques?', 'What behaviours?', 'Why these behaviours?'. Only then will you understand the desired level of skill, knowledge and expertise.

THE LEARNING GAP

Having conducted this analysis the trainer will have identified the learning gap, that is between the individual/team/organization's present and desired levels of capability. For a final check, test why this gap is present. This check should point you in the direction of the original business requirement. For example, it may be a change in business strategy that calls for different capabilities to achieve the new goals or an individual employee might be preparing for a job change which specifies additional skills or expertise. It pays to close the loop whenever possible.

2 HOW PEOPLE LEARN

Learning is what most adults will do for a living in the 21st Century
Lewis Perelman

In order to be a good trainer you need to understand how and why people learn. This chapter provides a brief introduction to learning theory. There have been many excellent books written on the subject during the past fifteen years. To explore this subject more fully I would refer you to D.A. Kolb, *Learning Style Inventory*, or P. Honey and A. Mumford, *Manual of Learning Styles*, as a starting point for individual learning styles, followed by P.M. Senge, *The Fifth Discipline*, which explores the 'learning organisation'. Over the years these formative works have inspired much further writing. Understanding your, and your trainees', learning style will enable you to make the most of your training interventions.

Kolb argues that there are four distinct stages in what he calls the learning cycle: Concrete Experiences (learning from feeling), Reflective Observation (learning from watching), Abstract Conceptualization (learning by thinking) and Active Experimentation (learning by doing). You will realize from the descriptions that no one style fits you completely. Your learning style is a combination of all four – you can adopt one or more learning styles in a given training situation. Consequently the design of a training event should provide opportunities for trainees to experience a variety of learning styles, so that all participants may learn in their preferred style.

Adults will usually learn if:

- they need to – there is a relevant and valid purpose behind the training
- they want to – there is a perceived benefit to the individual
- realistic problems are considered – training is practical, not theoretical
- progress can be measured – a real benefit can be seen by the trainee.

The learning experience is also enhanced if adult training is undertaken in a relatively informal atmosphere. The promotion of the concept that training is a joint learning experience (for to teach is to learn twice),

Cameo

Early in my consulting career I ran a skill development and problem-solving event for a construction company where the attendees were drawn from all levels of the organization. It was agreed that the event should be held off-site to reduce interruptions and I gave the managing director's assistant instructions concerning the room size and layout. On my arrival at the hotel I discovered that contrary to my request a very formal layout had been implemented, with name cards already in place that left no one in any doubt as to the status of each attendee. That action told me a great deal about the culture of the organization, particularly as their earlier words had not matched their actions. This layout was not going to help the learning experience so my co-trainer and I quickly removed the tables, gathered up the name cards and put them in a box to play a variant of 'Cinderella'*. When the delegates arrived half of them were issued with a name card other than their own, and requested to find their partner and commence the first exercise, 'Pictorial interview'. In this exercise, each trainee interviews their partner about their life outside work, then draws a picture on a piece of flipchart paper to aid their presentation to the main group. In this way some of the status issues were reduced as golf, photography and charity work were common activities to many of the delegates regardless of rank. The introductions were quickly followed by 'Sudden death'*, a large group problem-solving exercise designed to relax them. Only after this were we able to begin the planned event.

coupled with the reduction of any perceived teacher/pupil relationship between trainer and trainees, may be further developed by correct choice of location and layout of the training room.

Retention and recall

There has been a long-running debate about how much information is retained by our brain. The brain certainly has a massive storage capacity, of which we appear to use very little. Even in old age it still has immense capacity – many creative people continue to be prolific into advanced years. Given these facts the challenge for the trainer is to present material in such a way that in the first instance it is retained and, having been retained, can be recalled.

---

* See *75 Ways to Liven up Your Training.*

Exercise

Think back over the past year and write down five important events you can remember. Now look at the list and think about why you remembered each event. What happened? Why is it memorable? How much detail can you remember? Do you see any common themes emerging from the way your memory works? Check your thoughts against the list below.

1. Was the event at the beginning of a series of similar events?
2. Was the event at the end of a series of events?
3. Was it a bizarre or outstanding event?
4. Was the event linked to another event?
5. Was the event reviewed on one or more occasions?

Our mind makes linkages to help us remember. I am always surprised when I am trying to recall a person's name just how many linkages and information I have retained. For example, hair colour, eye colour, job, the clothes they were wearing, who else was there at the time . . . The more I think about it, the more links I make. Some of them may hinder my recall of the name as I shoot off at a tangent.

To aid training retention the following adage is absolutely true:

Tell them what you are going to tell them.
Tell them.
Tell them what you told them.

If, as you train, you can introduce something out of the ordinary to form a mental association or link you will have raised the likelihood of recall significantly. The film-maker Alfred Hitchcock used to introduce what he called a 'MacGuffin', a diversionary plot device, which, whilst it was meant to distract you, actually helped you to remember the story. In a similar way, a biology teacher used a member of the school's rugby team to explain muscle formation to the second year students – far more memorable than a textbook, in fact you could say that the lesson came alive.

Linking and using memorable events is only half the answer to recall and retention. High recall rates demand a regular review, for within one day a trainee will usually only remember about 25 per cent of the previous day's input. To keep the recall rate high you need to conduct reviews after one day, one week, one month and six months. After this time the material should have moved into long-term memory.

Cameo

One very successful trainer would organize the following reviews for a one-week course as follows.

During the delivery phase he would follow Kolb's learning styles by using a mixture of direct input, practical experimentation, a time for reflection and a brief end-of-day recap.

To help anchor the learning at the start of each day one team would review the previous day – the review had to be creative and not just a dull repetition. This tended to introduce another memorable event plus competition, for as the week went by the recaps became increasingly more creative.

On the last but one afternoon he included a role-play or similar exercise that incorporated many of the inputs of the week, including surprises that helped further to anchor some of the learnings.

On the last day he reviewed the exercise, recalling and anchoring the learnings again.

The last exercise of the week was the graffiti wall where learners wrote the memorable events of the week. This was photographed together with the group photograph.

This trainer encouraged the creation of self-help networks and set follow-up exercises, the results of which were circulated amongst the group.

After about a month participants received photographs of the group and the graffiti wall, again reminding them of the key points of the training event.

As a trainee I had the greatest retention and recall of any training event I had attended and when I was asked to train the course three years later I had little trouble in picking up the material and quickly developing a viable and healthy offspring.

Learning in groups

Much training is conducted within groups, often because it reflects the way we work in our organizations. However, learning in groups introduces a dynamic that must be allowed for when designing a training event. The main feature is that the trainer must consider both the social/maintenance and task dimensions of group work. Groups go through phases in their development and unless and until a group reaches a certain stage in its development then it is unlikely to attain high performance. There are many models available which describe the various phases a group goes through, e.g. Tuckman and Jenson's model is popular:

Forming   The 'sniffing out' or polite phase, where membership is defined, similarities and differences explored and there is likely to be confusion and ambiguity.

Storming   The control phase, where operating or decision-making rules are established, attempts are made to create order and leadership is contested.

Norming   The cohesion phase, where functional relationships have been determined and group member interdependence realized.

Performing   The high productivity phase, where collaboration and affection come to the forefront. There is group member synergy together with growth of both individuals and the group.

Adjourning   The closing down or mourning phase, where the task has been completed and the purpose of the group no longer exists.

The trainer must be able to recognize where the group is in its development in order to judge how much of the group's effort is being put into group maintenance and how much into the task. There could be little progress with the task set if all the group members' efforts are directed to maintenance tasks. The storming phase, in particular, demands high levels of energy and can be great fun or very stressful and threatening whilst the group attempts to determine roles and status. As a trainer, the main thing to remember is that productivity may be slow until the group issues are resolved. Do not be surprised if output is lower from a group compared to an individual undertaking a similar task. The individual is not concerned with group processes or communications.

Improving communication within the group

Lack of trust and feeling threatened has a distorting effect on communication within the group. If honest and meaningful communications are to be established the group must:

1. Develop a sense of mutual trust and openness.
2. Use constructive feedback to correct communication distortions.
3. Discuss the process of communication.

Attention must be paid to these guidelines if the group is to communicate effectively. Individuals must be willing:

- to be open and honest themselves about their own feelings
- to be open and honest by discreetly disclosing their feelings to others
- to listen to feedback and then decide on an appropriate action.

I have found the 'Johari Window' model (Luft 1970) a useful device for analysing and working on these problems. It was developed by *Jo* Luft and *Harry* Ingham, hence its name. It comprises four quadrants (see Figure 2.1):

Quadrant 1: the open area or public self – behaviour which is known to self and others.

Quadrant 2: the blind area – what others can see but of which we are unaware.

Quadrant 3: the hidden area or private self – things we prefer to keep to ourselves, e.g. very personal feelings or hidden agendas.

Quadrant 4: the unknown area – neither accessible to us nor to others, i.e. behaviour that affects our relationships without our knowing it.

Luft suggests that any change in the size of one quadrant will affect the others. For example, arrow 1 indicates where feedback has been given:

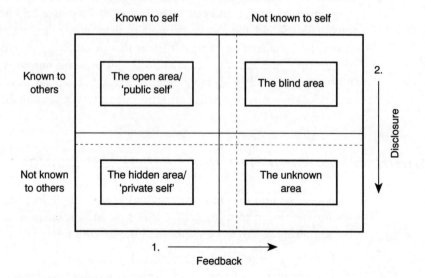

Figure 2.1 The Johari Window

'You always jangle your keys when you present', which moves the vertical line to the right. In the same way if you disclose, arrow 2, something about yourself: 'I am a stickler for detail', the horizontal line moves downwards. The diagram indicates that with sensitive disclosure and feedback the unknown area, which may also impact relationships, is reduced. This model is both easy to understand and powerful in helping group members to communicate better.

Because the giving and receiving of feedback is the cornerstone of the model here are a few simple rules that will help to promote healthy communication.

GIVING FEEDBACK

- Timing is of the essence. Give feedback as soon as possible after the particular behaviour, but before proceeding always consider the social situation and the receiver's readiness to receive feedback.

- Be descriptive, non-judgemental and specific. Describing what you feel or hear reduces the need for the receiver to behave defensively.

- Disclose your own feelings or position vis-à-vis the other person: 'I get very upset when you say . . .'. Be sensitive; do not dump your feelings on others.

- Consider both your needs and the needs of the receiver. *Feedback should be for the benefit of the receiver, not the giver.*

- Test that the message is understood. Ask the receiver to paraphrase what you have just said to check if that was what you meant.

- In a group situation allow the giver and receiver the opportunity to check with others in the group on the feedback's accuracy.

- Feedback should not be imposed. 'Let ME give YOU some FEEDBACK!' rarely works. Start with a discussion about giving and receiving and let it flow from there. The build up of trust within the group will improve communications.

RECEIVING FEEDBACK

- Listen to the person who is giving the feedback.

- Try to understand their feelings and accept that what they are saying is genuine.

- You do not have to modify your behaviour. Give the feedback serious consideration; weigh up the consequences of changing or not changing.

- Express your own feelings and thoughts to the giver and communicate your decisions to the giver.

- Tell the giver what they can do which might help you change.

- Thank the giver for their concern and help.

Feedback is the surest way to improve our communications within the group and if it is undertaken with honesty and care significant changes can be achieved. The trainer can help in the early stages by explaining the model and being available to facilitate should the group require it. Do not impose yourself on the group and remember that you have feelings as well.

3 EVENT DESIGN

If I had not lifted up the stone, you had not found the jewel.

Hebrew Proverb

Clearly the ways in which we learn, communicate, remember and recall will have a significant influence on the way you design training. Wherever possible the training design should incorporate the different learning styles and include strategies which will increase the likelihood of information retention. Before we examine the details of designing a training event it is worth considering the many different approaches to people development. Some of those listed below can be designed into the event to allow change of pace and style.

Training techniques

There are many techniques/approaches available to the trainer. Ten of them are set out below, together with some of their attendant advantages and disadvantages.

LECTURE

A lecture is a structured talk, usually accompanied by visual aids, e.g. OHP foils, flipchart, and slides.

Advantages Suitable for large audiences where participation is not required. It allows for the content and timing to be planned in detail in advance.

Disadvantages A lively presentation style is needed, with regular changes of pace and media for successful delivery. Low levels of interaction and feedback may make it difficult to assess what has been communicated.

CASE STUDY

A case study is a written examination/description of a situation, often based on real life, which encourages learning by analysing the case, defining the problem(s) and proposing solution(s).

Cameo

A needs analysis undertaken for a scientific/engineering organization indicated that its administrative staff, who were the initial customer contact point, required a better appreciation of the work undertaken by their technical colleagues and a basic understanding of the technical terms used within the industry.

The training solution design included:

- a non-technical lecture, using analogies to explain the basic principles that underpinned the technology
- an easy-to-watch video that demonstrated and explained the technology and technical terms used
- a lecture by an experienced technical manager explaining the technical terms in more detail and describing the role of the technician and how it related to the administrators' jobs (layman's language was used throughout the presentation with tape recordings to further illustrate the technical terms)
- a playlet followed by group discussion and mini lecture focusing on customer care and management
- a role-reversal activity where the administrators undertook some of the activities of a technician
- a series of role-plays where the administrators received customer calls, some of which were of a technical nature.

The six approaches built on each other to give a gradual progression into the technical arena, whilst also satisfying the various learning styles of the participants. Feedback at the end of the event indicated that the design had very successfully met the administrators' training needs.

Advantages Opportunities for analysis and individual or group discussion on key points of case and problem solving.

Disadvantages May be difficult in a large group situation. May oversimplify the true complexity or political climate of a situation.

ROLE-PLAY

The enacting of roles in a 'safe' training environment.

Advantages Face-to-face situations, if correctly set up, allow the participant to experience a full range of emotions. Enables rapid trainer and/or co-participant feedback/coaching plus the opportunity to try again.

Cameo

A geographically spread UK organization discovered that, even though there were well documented policies and procedures, each local office performed the business processes almost entirely differently. On investigation it was discovered that all training had been conducted by 'Sitting with Nellie', and that over the years more and more 'special case' local procedures had been introduced so there was no consistency across the UK. The solution was to review the current procedures, redesign the processes and centrally retrain all the staff in these revised processes. This in turn provided an opportunity to deliver some key messages about the future direction of the organization and obtain attendees' views on the proposed strategy. Further training events were planned for new staff and a forum for all staff was created so they could continue to monitor and review the processes on a UK basis rather than unilaterally.

Advantages Little or no direct training cost. The trainee may almost immediately start making a contribution to the team's performance goals etc. It may help introducing a new member to the team.

Disadvantages Nellie may be incapable of coherently explaining how he/she undertakes the job. Reduced output from 'Nellie' whilst helping the trainee. Bad habits may be transferred from 'Nellie' to the trainee. The trainee may not see the wider organizational picture.

Internal or external courses and/or trainers

There are a number of possible permutations when considering whether to hold an event internally or externally and whether to use in-house or external trainers to deliver the event.

INTERNAL

Individuals from the same organization are brought together for development.

Advantages The content can be made directly relevant to the organization and can help promote a common message (see cameo above). It is easier to integrate the event into a broader staff development or change programme and large numbers of people can be trained at one time.

Disadvantages No exposure to new ideas or approaches from fellow participants outside of the organization. It can provide a platform for group moans about the organization (see 'Dealing with difficult situations', p. 69).

EXTERNAL

An event attended by people from a variety of organizations.
Advantages Attendees have an opportunity to meet new people and to be exposed to new ideas and thinking.
Disadvantages Content may be too general or, worse still, evangelical without providing the tools and skills to bring about the desired change. Many of these courses can be very expensive.

IN-HOUSE TRAINERS

Trainers who are drawn from within the organization. They may or may not be members of the personnel or training functions.
Advantages These trainers should understand the organization and its culture and be able to relate the training to the organizational needs. Direct costs should be lower as they are already on the payroll and they may be quicker at responding than an external trainer.
Disadvantages They may be too familiar with the people being trained and may not necessarily be good role models. If not trained in teaching skills they may be technically sound but poor at putting it across. If training represents only a small part of their role it may be given insufficient time for preparation, i.e. the presenters do it 'off the cuff' rather than preparing properly. Remember the saying: 'If you "wing it", don't be surprised when you are shot down'.

EXTERNAL TRAINERS

Bringing people in from outside to deliver the course. Such people might be called trainers, advisors, or consultants and may be independent sole traders or employees/associates of a large consulting or training organization.
Advantages Higher levels of skill and competence in the subject area than internal staff (if not, why are they being employed?). Time to develop the materials and no political axe to grind.
Disadvantages They may need to learn about your organization and/or the market in which you operate. They can be expensive and may deliver pre-packaged training that is not a good fit to your organization's needs.

Cameo

A training department had neither the technical skills nor the resources to undertake an important training initiative in support of organizational change. Its solution was to contract in a skilled course designer and trainer to undertake the needs analysis and prepare an outline course design. In parallel two 'technical' staff were sent on a two-day course where they were introduced to the basic training concepts. They then worked with the contractor who coached them in course design and delivery whilst he developed the course materials. This coaching and knowledge transfer continued with the two designated staff and with the other presenters at rehearsals and during the event itself. During the event the contractor also acted in the role of an independent facilitator. At the end of each course the contractor provided feedback together with hints and tips as to how performance might be improved. By the end of the series the two 'technical' staff had significantly developed their training skills and the other presenters had improved their presentation skills. Also, the course was seen as owned by the two technical staff who received very high ratings from the trainees for its design and delivery.

It is apparent from the above pros and cons that bringing in someone from outside to support a training initiative requires careful consideration. You will need to ascertain from them:

- precisely what they are offering – approach, style and materials
- who is delivering the training – you must see the actual trainers
- what learning methods they will employ
- what materials they will use
- who else they have done similar work for – talk to someone from that organization
- that they will adapt their materials to meet your specific needs
- that they have empathy with your organization, its goals and those being trained
- that they are really interested in this work. Are they willing to invest some of their time before the contract is awarded?
- precisely how much it will cost – watch out for expenses.

Involve the line management of the trainees in the selection process and when talking to external trainer(s) try to judge their competence and subject area knowledge and how they will put this knowledge across. A mixture of informal discussion and formal presentation can reveal interesting insights. Finally ask yourself:

- Do I feel comfortable with this person?
- Does the proposal meet my needs?
- Does it represent good value for money?

If you cannot say a confident 'Yes' to each of these three questions do not issue a contract. Elicit additional information and/or reconsider the original needs analysis.

4 THE EXCELLENT TRAINER

A good specialist can explain things as complicated as they exactly are. A good trainer can explain with simplicity how manageable things are. *

If someone says to you 'I am a trainer', what sort of picture does it conjure up? Is it someone who stands at the front of a lecture theatre or perhaps facilitates a business game, or do they help horses win races or enable tigers to jump through hoops of fire? Many roles or activities are encompassed within the word, some of which are appropriate to our discussion and others less so. For as language has evolved so have the labels that are applied. The football managers and trainers of the 1970s are today football coaches and assistant coaches. I know of one multinational corporation who decided to follow the football example and renamed several of its senior managers as coaches. Although the sentiment may have been correct, the behaviours of some of the managers did not change with their change of name. One executive aptly summed up the situation: 'In Britain a coach is something with eight wheels and 45 seats travelling at 70 miles per hour on the motorway. It would be foolish to get in its way.' I do not believe this was the type of behaviour which was intended by the CEO. The statement clearly shows, however, the need to develop your people's skills and behaviours, even the senior managers', in line with any proposed organizational change.

The term people developer came into vogue for a while during the 1980s and early 90s. People developer, whilst describing what the role entails, still failed to conjure up a consistent vision of its attributes. But what does a trainer look like to you?

Exercise   On a sheet of A4 paper draw a cartoon picture of what you think a trainer should look like.

What does your cartoon show? Does it have a big mouth for talking? Or perhaps a shield for deflecting difficult questions? Or thick skin? What

---

* After Ioan Tenner, whose skill, knowledge and enthusiasm for the subject was a key factor in my following a people development career path.

about some of the other skills, like empathy – how have you portrayed those attributes? As Shakespeare's Juliet says: 'A rose by any other name would smell as sweet'. With that in mind I will focus on how a trainer or people developer 'smells', rather than worry about what he or she is called by the organization.

What combination of personal characteristics, skills, knowledge and experience does the organization require of the *excellent* trainer? Your cartoon may have identified many of them. Here are some worth considering.

Personal attributes

'By your words they will know you, by your deeds they will judge you.'

The *excellent* trainer:

- is a person of integrity
- is physically fit
- creates and meets high expectations
- is widely experienced
- has impact
- is prepared to learn from the students
- practises what is taught
- is self-motivated
- communicates effectively
- is aware of the feeling of others
- believes in him/herself and the role
- questions and listens effectively
- assimilates and applies new information
- adapts to new or changing situations
- manages problems
- remains calm and objective in all situations
- modifies his/her style or approach as required
- plans and organizes.

INTEGRITY

The trainer's integrity goes beyond honesty or soundness. It is more to do with maintaining the ethical standards of the role. A trainer can often be in a position of power in relation to his/her students. He/she may also hear and see things during exercises or even whilst everyone is relaxing in the bar. Power should not be abused, nor should tales be told. There is only one exception to this rule: when there is a formal contract in place to feed back performance or behavioural information to a delegate's manager. Such a contract must be three-way and open. You should never contract to provide feedback without the delegate's prior knowledge and agreement. Delegate trust is a main element of successful training events, particularly if you are working on behavioural skills. Without integrity there will be little trust.

FITNESS

Running effective training events is a demanding role. A trainer can be on the go from early in the morning until late at night. As you already appreciate, the role entails bringing about change in the delegates, whether it is learning a new skill or modifying their behaviour. When change occurs there is always some associated stress. The fitter you are, the better your ability to cope with any stressful situations. When running residential courses it can be very easy to eat and drink to excess, particularly at luxury hotels. When you are socializing with the delegates watch the calories and alcohol units. Use the hotel pool or gym at every opportunity.

HIGH EXPECTATIONS

Setting and achieving high expectations demands a twofold approach. The first is student focused and the second is self-directed. At the start of the event realistic goals that stretch the students should be agreed and the trainer's role is to see that these are met. Secondly, you should always set yourself a personal goal. Success is your greatest enemy. It can be very tempting, when you have run a successful event on a number of occasions, to coast and just enjoy it. After all you worked very hard to make the event a success and now it is only fair to ease up for a bit. Unfortunately such an approach will take the 'edge' off the event and, if you are not careful, it will be downhill all the way.

I was once told about a fish farm whose salmon looked appetizing enough, but did not taste quite like netted or line caught ones. The owner tried changing their diet, water, condition etc., but there was no improvement in quality. Then one day he thought of the idea of introducing a predator into the farm. He lost a few fish to the predator but the quality of the others became excellent as they swam around trying to avoid being eaten. If you constantly set yourself new challenges, perhaps by changing the seating layout or modifying an exercise, the quality of the event will continue to remain excellent.

WIDELY EXPERIENCED

Training is concerned with the acquisition of new skills and knowledge. There are times when students may become blocked or even lethargic when learning. A wide experience of life not only provides a good understanding of people and human behaviour, but also supplies a rich resource of knowledge. By introducing an appropriate anecdote or metaphor you will be able to reduce blockages and make a subject more interesting. *Excellent* trainers are naturally curious people who are interested in a wealth of things, not just their training speciality.

IMPACT

Start your training event with a 'bang'. The impact will create a good first impression, but you must maintain that first impression. Impact will enable you to sell yourself and then quickly gain attention and credibility. Remember: 'You never get a second chance to make a first impression'. I once saw a poster in a Parisian office showing two Wild West gun fighters in a 'stand off' above that particular saying. Even though my French was poor I immediately understood and remembered the message. Images can add impact to the message.

LEARNS FROM STUDENTS

Training is a two-way communication, unlike a television programme or video. Over the years I have found that my most successful training events were usually very interactive, with students providing a fresh insight or new perspective to the subject. It is likely that your students can provide useful feedback, both positive and negative, about the subject and/or your performance. Always acknowledge all inputs and, unless there is strong evidence to the contrary, accept all comments as honest and true contributions to the learning experience. However, you do not have to embrace all contributions immediately. First evaluate the input critically and, if you accept the observations, modify your behaviour or the course content accordingly. Having accepted the change the *excellent* trainer will quickly assimilate and apply the information.

PRACTISES WHAT IS TAUGHT

In the early stages of skill development trainees often like to observe how the task or activity is performed before attempting it themselves. You may not be the perfect role model but your actions and behaviours should at the very least be congruent with what is being taught. 'Do as I say, not as I do' is unacceptable training practice. An obvious example is a presentation skills trainer who breaks many of the rules for making a good presentation whilst training the subject.

SELF-MOTIVATED

Training is a demanding activity, both physically and emotionally. It is not unusual for trainers to feel drained or even bruised after a particularly tough day. Thus, the first element of self-motivation is that no matter how hard the previous session was you enter the next one full of energy and vitality. However, just as important as the 'show must go on' approach is the continual striving for the better way of delivering the training experience. 'There must be a better way' should be the trainer's watchwords. Be positive and expect to succeed in finding that better way. Let negative feedback or anxieties push you forward rather than hold you back. If you find it difficult to motivate yourself then work with someone who will push you along. Should none of these solutions work for you, consider changing your career. Students will soon recognize the unmotivated trainer and your training will rapidly become a sort of hell on earth.

COMMUNICATES EFFECTIVELY

Good communication is the cornerstone of successful training. It should be jargon free, appropriate to the audience, clear, precise and concise. Take care with your language, particularly everyday English. For example, consider the word 'love'. We love our dog, we love our spouse, we love pizza, we love the Beatles etc. We love everything. In Latin there are over 20 words describing different types of love. Is it any wonder people have trouble understanding and communicating? In Chapter 2 we saw that students learn in a variety of ways and a number of communication styles and media may have to be adopted to transfer the skill or knowledge. Other attributes for successful communication, like impact, being aware of others' feelings, cultural differences, questioning and listening, are discussed at various points throughout the book.

AWARE OF FEELINGS

Human beings are sensitive creatures and when establishing rapport you should show both respect and concern. Do this in an empathetic rather than sympathetic manner. It is rather like walking in their shoes. You must also consider your own needs and feelings before taking any action. Failure to engage with yourself will, in the long run, have a dysfunctional effect on the trainer/student relationship. What ever action you take should preserve the student's self-esteem and maintain a good working relationship. This style of approach will help you create a positive atmosphere and foster the correct level of relationship for effective learning.

BELIEVES IN HIM/HERSELF AND THE ROLE

There are two sides to this element: having a positive self-image and being committed. A positive self-image is a prerequisite to successfully undertaking the training role. Being committed means you will make the extra effort to achieve success on behalf of your students without putting self-interest first. The following tale helps to distinguish between involvement and commitment.

One day a chicken and a pig were discussing how they might set up in business together. They looked at each of their available resources and agreed to form a partnership to sell egg and bacon breakfast to night workers at the end of their shifts. As you can readily see, the chicken was involved in the venture, but the pig was committed.

QUESTIONS AND LISTENS EFFECTIVELY

Questioning and listening are fundamental to effective oral communication. You must be able to formulate and ask appropriate questions and listen actively to the reply. A good question that eases learning will:

- be relevant to the subject matter
- limited to one thought (more than one thought may confuse)
- be brief
- begin with an interrogatory word or phrase (who, what, when, where, why, how)
- be carefully phrased.

Expert listening is a challenging skill. You have to look for both the context and content, that is the feeling and language used as well as the facts contained in the communication. You often have to hunt for the golden nugget and having found it the *excellent* trainer will check that his/her understanding is correct.

ASSIMILATES AND APPLIES NEW INFORMATION

Knowledge is continually expanding and information moves with increasing rapidity around the globe. Search for appropriate information, check its relevance and integrate it into your existing understanding. Do not dismiss any knowledge that contradicts your existing understanding, but probe and examine it deeply. If the new knowledge is relevant to you, modify your models and frameworks accordingly.

ADAPTS TO NEW OR CHANGING SITUATIONS

Changes of people, tasks or environments may occur during a training course or series of courses. The changes may be significant or even sudden. No matter what happens, you must strive to maintain your effectiveness. When changes occur, particularly unexpectedly, the *excellent* trainer always looks for serendipity. If you look for serendipity in these situations – you will almost always find it.

MANAGES PROBLEMS

When faced with a potential problem first identify and isolate the problem, then seek appropriate data to help you understand the issues. Only then can you diagnose the possible causes and decide on a plan of action. Inexperienced trainers will make unsubstantiated assumptions or move straight from recognizing that there is a problem to action.

Cameo

Some years ago I observed a trainer with high control needs who was suddenly put into an 'out of control' situation. Her students had presented a piece of work that contradicted all of her teachings from the previous two days. It was meant to be humorous, but unfortunately the trainer thought it was a personal attack. Her instinctive reaction was to lash out orally at the 'assailants', which took them completely by surprise and caused deep shock to all concerned. Unfortunately, this was the only event from the course that most of them remembered.

REMAINS CALM AND OBJECTIVE

A logical, unbiased and rational approach is the way to handle difficult personal attacks. The *excellent* trainer will control his/her response by not reacting emotionally to provocation. Always prepare a strategy in advance to allow you to think through such a situation and respond appropriately. When shocked it is useful to count to ten and count again before saying or doing anything.

MODIFIES STYLE AND APPROACH

Trainer flexibility is important. You may have to modify your teaching approach to match different student requirements or, having recognized resistance, apathy or unexpected behaviours, change your plan so that the underlying issues can be discussed and resolved. Be sensitive.

PLANS AND ORGANIZES

As a trainer always establish appropriate courses of action for your students and yourself so that they achieve the identified learning gaols. Prepare implementation plans and identify the necessary actions to ensure that goals are attained. Determine your priorities and develop a realistic plan in terms of timing and resourcing. Build in contingencies to allow for possible resource constraints and unexpected events and once the plan is agreed monitor and manage its implementation.

Skills

The personal attributes are the foundations on which excellent skills are built. The *excellent* trainer will be skilled in:

- presenting – using all 'platform' skills as and when appropriate
- coaching – helping to develop individual and team/group skills
- facilitating – easing the group processes in achieving their learning goal
- leadership – motivating and offering direction and support towards a goal
- counselling – helping individuals overcome learning problems.

The *excellent* trainer will mix and match these skills, as appropriate, when helping students to achieve their learning goals.

Many of these skills will be examined in more detail in Part II, 'Running a Successful Training Event'.

PART 2

RUNNING A SUCCESSFUL TRAINING EVENT

Drawn by Simon Jarvis

A journey of a thousand miles must begin with a single step.

Lao Tzu

Undertaking the needs analysis and converting it into an innovative design which precisely meets the organization's training requirements are but the first steps to delivering a successful event. There is still much to be done before you take your place at the 'lectern' to welcome the participants. Your aim must be to *load the event for success*. Below are three rules (based on Herbert Shepherd) which, if followed, should help weigh the outcome in your favour.

Rule 1. *Stay alive and keep optimistic*

Let your whole self be involved in the undertaking, be in touch with yourself and your purpose. Carefully weigh up the risks – are they part of a purposeful strategy? When you are alive you are using your skills, knowledge and emotions to best effect and are not used by them. Do not allow yourself to become trapped in other people's games, in win–lose situations or wasting time with defensive manoeuvring. You are alive when you see dilemmas as opportunities for creativity, greet absurdity with laughter and capture the moment in the light of the future. You see and measure everything through the eyes of your purpose. Be positive and optimistic in your dealings with the client's organization so you can help them change the present and thereby create a new future.

Rule 2. *Start where the client is*

The empathy rule. To communicate effectively you must understand how the client (trainee and/or manager etc.) sees himself and his situation. The phrase 'to walk a mile in their shoes' sums it up well. The resulting relationship can be one of mutual support but take care not to become dependent upon each other.

Rule 3. *Work smart*

Do not work in ways which build resistance and always look for the most promising area to work in. Wherever possible use 'friends' who are keen and interested for the pilot courses, not people who first have to be convinced of the reason they are there before you start to train them. If you can, work with a partner or as a team member rather than alone. Choose them carefully, pick people whose ideas are congruent to your own. In the early days of a project always dedicate more resources than you would ever believe necessary for the project's success. This is based on the old military adage that you need three times as many forces to attack than the defenders can muster. Finally, do not argue if you cannot win. But if you have to use confrontation to win, make sure you have plenty of support.

5 BEFORE THE EVENT

Know how to ask. There is nothing more difficult for some people. Nor for others easier.

Baltasar Gracian

A training event is no different from any other public performance of, say, a play or orchestral concert. Just gathering together a group of actors or musicians and putting them in the auditorium a few moments before the performance is likely to result in a memorable event – but not one they or you would wish to be remembered by. As you will readily appreciate, there is a great deal of work done by all involved in the enterprise before the play or concert is performed, particularly when it is a première. This struck a chord powerfully with me when I was staying for a few days at the same hotel as a symphony orchestra. Each morning, as I walked down the corridor to my room, I would hear a variety of different instrumental sounds emanating from each musician's room as they practised alone. After lunch they would meet for a rehearsal lasting two or three hours and then, after a break, for that evening's performance. The conductor and players were leaving nothing to chance – good preparation was the key to their success.

Similarly the three most important factors for a successful training event are preparation, preparation and preparation.

- Preparing the people.
- Preparing the venue.
- Preparing the materials.

Following this advice lays firm foundations which will ensure success.

Preparing the people

How many 'Johns' (see the cameo overleaf) attend courses whose managers have:

- not checked the event's relevance to the trainee and job?

Cameo

> Towards the end of the second day of a week-long skills course it was apparent to all concerned, particularly in the work group, that John was deliberately being disruptive. The group had tried to explore the problem but had made little progress and it became necessary for the course leader to intervene before the situation became destructive. The leader took John to one side and over a beer tried to understand his behaviour. John easily fulfilled the skill, knowledge and experience prerequisites and had the intellectual capability to cope with the concepts and experiences that were being explored and yet he had continually been disruptive.
>
> The discussion revealed that John had been sent on the course because his manager thought it would be appropriate for his personal development. There had been no discussion with his manager concerning those 'needs', nor had John been briefed as to the nature of the event he was attending. Consequently John could not understand the relevance of the course and the only outcome he could see was that by attending he would probably miss a project deadline unless he worked all weekend and very long hours during the next week. He felt angry and frustrated and was taking it out on his team members. The discussion continued over a couple more pints, exploring a number of issues John faced, and it was agreed that his best strategy was to leave the course the following morning.

- not discussed it with the individual?
- not understood what the course is about?

How many 'Johns' have:

- not known what the training is about?
- felt indifferent or even hostile to the learning experience?

Or attended because:

- of the course's good reputation, whether the development is needed or not?
- they have some training days that must be used up before the end of the year (their right)?

The consequences of such behaviour are that the experience will be negative and that time and money will have been wasted.

Successful training is founded on a three-way contract between manager, trainee and trainer. Exactly how the contracting takes place will generally depend on the number of internal processes within the organization, which follow on from the identification of a development need. The trainer must ensure that the manager and trainee are involved in the process.

The manager may have identified the development need and might also have been involved in suggesting or formulating a solution. The manager may have even nominated the member of staff for training. In this case it should be relatively straightforward for the manager to perform his/her part of the contract. If this is not the case the manager will have to research the need and the proposed solution before taking any action. There may be company policies and procedures that describe the process and, just as important, rules concerning travel and expenses. The learning experience can be spoilt if the trainee is constantly worrying about money. Providing advances or tickets/warrants can ease the financial burden and the mind of employees, particularly the more junior ones.

THE MANAGER'S PART OF THE CONTRACT

- Discuss the development need with the member of staff (trainee) before applying for the training. (If your organization uses a training nomination form it may provide some prompts for the discussion. An example of a training nomination form can be found in the Compendium at the end of this book.)
- Brief the trainee before the training event takes place. (If your organization issues joining instructions they may provide some prompts for the discussion. An example of a set of joining instructions is included in the Compendium.)
- Debrief the trainee after the training event has taken place. (If your organization uses a training evaluation form it may provide some prompts for discussion. A model training evaluation form is shown in the Compendium.)
- Check that the trainee will have the opportunity to use the skill and/or knowledge after the event.
- Provide coaching to help develop the skill.

When briefing the trainee before the course the manager should explain:

- the reasons for attending the course – link to development needs, appraisals or own request
- what the course will involve in terms of broad content and learning style, e.g. outward bound, communications skills, team working

Cameo

A customer skills course had been arranged for an international company. One week before the course the company announced widespread redundancies. As a consequence of this management action 25 per cent of chosen trainees were advised that their services would no longer be required in about three months. The tone and flavour of the event changed significantly and it took a great deal of skill and energy on the part of the trainers plus a significant amount of counselling to keep the course on target. In retrospect one can see that the event should probably have been cancelled.

- how the training will be applied and link in to the trainee's continuing development
- when and where the event is taking place and, if required, an explanation of travel arrangements, accommodation, expenses and advances of expenses
- whether or not there is any reporting back.

If there are any questions that cannot be answered the manager should contact the trainer or the personnel department for an explanation.

The manager will provide the trainer prior to the event with background information on:

- the trainees, their jobs, experience and skills
- any concerns about the trainees
- what is happening in the organization and any current or potential issues that might be raised during the training.

THE TRAINER'S PART OF THE CONTRACT

- Brief the manager as to the nature and style of the event.
- Advise of any prerequisites, e.g. previous training courses that must have been attended, skill level, fitness.
- Agree whether or not there will be feedback on trainee performance and what form it will take. (The trainee must also agree to this before attending the event. If there is a request for a considerable amount of feedback, the trainer should define its purpose with the manager. Training events do not often make good assessment centres unless the assessment has been specifically built in to the event.)

THE TRAINEE'S PART OF THE CONTRACT

- Approach the training event with an open mind.
- Make the best endeavours to learn.
- Try to apply the learning after the event.
- Provide honest feedback as to the quality and relevance of the event.

Preparing the venue

Assume nothing. To do so can make an ASS of U and ME.

Anon.

After the skill, knowledge and experience of its leaders, the venue is the next most important element of any learning event. It will be 'home' for a few days, or possibly weeks, and if it is unsuitable it may significantly impair the learning experience. Overhead projectors breaking down or even lost handouts are often tolerated by delegates, but a cramped, hot (or cold) stuffy room with uncomfortable seats is likely to cause dissent within an hour or two.

Over the years I have had the misfortune of participating in events with the most unsuitable of environments. At one the air conditioning malfunctioned. The temperature soared to over 32°C which, when combined with a good lunch and a darkened room, made it virtually impossible for the delegates to stay awake, let alone learn anything. At another event the hotel had misread the room measurement units and provided a 15 × 10 feet room instead of the 15 × 10 metre one requested. It was a 'very friendly' learning experience.

If you are holding a training event in a new location, never ASSUME anything. Whenever possible visit the location during the planning phase of the event. If this is impracticable, ask the hotel or conference centre to send you plans and photographs of the rooms they are proposing you use. Explain your requirements in writing and always confirm in writing what has been agreed orally. Be just as specific about any breakout or team rooms you will be using. Hotels often temporarily convert bedrooms for this purpose and they can prove to be too small for a team of six. Finally, check your own bedroom. Leading a learning event can be exhausting and you will need a restful night's sleep. Avoid any room near the lift or above the hotel tradesmen's entrance. Being woken at 4.30 am to the sound of kitchen porters unloading a lorry is not the best preparation for your high-energy day ahead. This advice applies equally to the delegates' rooms; you also want them 'raring to go'.

Meal and coffee/tea breaks can also be traps for the unwary. Some sessions may not start and finish precisely when you planned. It is a good idea to allow a degree of flexibility for the meal and drink break timings with the venue management in advance of the event. Even so, be sensitive to their needs of running a business – arriving an hour late for lunch is unlikely to foster good relationships. Let the venue management know as early as possible if a session is running significantly late so that it will reduce the impact to the agreed domestic arrangements. Most venue managers will do their best to accommodate you, provided they are told what is happening early enough. Avoid alcohol at lunchtime if possible. Following some bad experiences I always instruct the venues to provide a light lunch accompanied by soft drinks and water. Such a request is sometimes not viewed sympathetically in continental Europe. Be sensible – one glass of wine with a meal is unlikely to dull the senses.

Finally, most venues will supply flipcharts, pens, paper and audio-visual equipment etc. Confirm precisely with the venue management what they are providing and whether it is included in the price of the facility. The supply of audio-visual equipment can prove to be a very expensive extra, as can extra bottles of water, cakes and fruit. Telephones in the main or breakout rooms should have a bar on outside lines. On occasions some unscrupulous delegates, in an attempt to control their own company's costs, may use these telephones for business and even personal calls, leaving the organizers to foot the bill at the end of the event. If the venue management set up a general account code for the event make sure that you are the only person able to sign for any extras, be it photocopying or wine. Set these controls before the start of the event and you will not find yourself having to pay for more than you expected at the end.

The following checklist will prompt you to ask the correct questions when planning the event and help to provide a satisfactory learning environment:

- Venue contact name(s) and where to find them
- Earliest access time prior to event start
- Latest departure time after event close
- Correct size main and breakout rooms
- Appropriate seating patterns
- Good writing surfaces for delegates (where applicable)
- Comfortable chairs
- Thermostatically controlled temperature (ideally 18°–20°C)
- Controlled ventilation – air conditioning or windows
- Adequate sound-proofing

- Able to isolate/switch off venue broadcast systems
- Lighting – natural, blinds/curtains
- Audio-visual equipment, flipcharts, pens and paper
- Location of power points and light switches
- Central electrical controls for lights and A/V, etc.
- Agreed domestic arrangements – meal and break times
- Message delivery arrangements
- Telephone barring
- Accounting and sign-off procedures

SEATING ARRANGEMENTS

The size of room will greatly influence the seating arrangement. Determine how you wish to arrange the seating during the design and planning stages of the event, remembering that the arrangement adopted can affect both the event's style and delegate interaction. In some instances the room size might dictate the only suitable seating layout and you will have to be flexible in your approach. Some venue managements have their own ideas about how a room should be organized, even though they have been advised in advance. I have often had to resort to moving the seating myself to obtain the desired effect. Try experimenting with the seating arrangements. It can bring a new and interesting dimension to an event you have run many times before. When planning the seating remember that:

- rows of seats reduce interaction between delegates
- delegates at the back will usually participate less than those at front
- delegates will usually try to sit in the same seat for all sessions
- reorganizing the seating patterns between sessions can be upsetting for the delegates
- disaffected delegates will often sit at the back or even away from the main group.

U or horseshoe shape

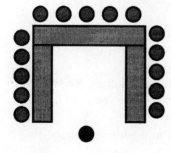

Advantages

- Delegates can see each other and communicate easily.
- The leader can walk into the U and interact with each delegate.
- Commonly used layout which is non-threatening to delegates.
- Works well for groups of 20 people or less.

Disadvantages

- Formal arrangement (see variation.)
- Distance between each side of U may inhibit interaction.
- Distance may be too great from back of U to OHP screen or flipchart.
- Delegates near the front may have to twist round by more than 60° to see screen.
- The positioning of audio-visual equipment can mask some delegates.

Variation

- An open U (i.e. no desks in front of delegates) makes the arrangement less formal. Use when high interaction is required, e.g. behavioural skill development events.

Lecture theatre or parallel rows

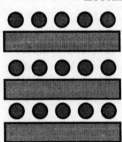

Advantages

- Excellent use of available space.
- Delegates have clear view of audio-visuals. (Rear rows may need to be elevated.)
- Good for lecture-style presentations.

Disadvantages

- Very poor interaction between delegates.
- Poor interaction between leader and delegates.
- May need a purpose-built room to obtain the advantages.

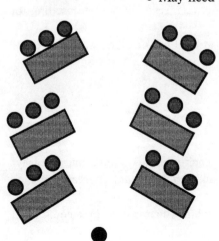

Chevron or herringbone

Place rows at an angle of about 60°–90° with a centre aisle between them.

Advantages

- Not as restricting as parallel rows arrangement.
- All delegates are at a good angle for screens.
- Leader can walk down the 'spine' to interact with delegates.
- Good with groups in a confined space.

Disadvantages

- Difficult for delegates to see each other.
- Delegates' view of screens masked by others.
- Reduces group interaction.

Variation

- V shaped, i.e. one row only. Gives optimum leader/delegate interaction with good visibility, but is suitable for small groups (10 or less delegates) only.

Cluster or bistro
Four to seven people at a table.

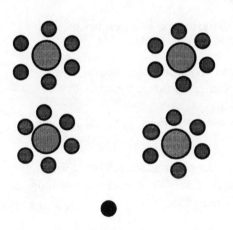

Advantages

- Good for large groups.
- Ideal for team building.
- Allows some participation between tables.
- Small group work possible without moving.
- Leader can move between groups and join groups if appropriate.

Disadvantages

- Difficult for all delegates to see the leader or screens without turning.
- Encourages small group conversations during presentations.
- Can result in large group becoming fragmented.

Conference table

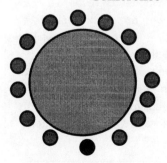

Advantages

- Good for small groups or meetings.
- Prompts interactive discussion.

Disadvantages

- If more than 15 delegates the distance between them becomes too great.

- 'Head of the table' issues can emerge – a round table is best.

Preparing the materials

How do you choose the materials and/or equipment that will support the training? In an ideal world, to create conditions to help people learn you would select the most appropriate aids to meet the variety of learning approaches used during your training event. However, the following practical constraints have to be faced.

- the timescale in which the training has to be designed and delivered
- the resources you can draw upon – equipment, materials and people
- the size of your training event budget
- your familiarity with the medium.

Remember that we receive and store information in a number of ways. We can:

- see it – using our mind's eye we can recall pictures, images, charts
- hear it – using our mind's ear we can recall tunes, sounds, conversations, accents
- feel it – using our feelings we can recall emotions, taste/smell, tactile experiences, pain

We each have a preferred channel for the input and recall of information. The excellent trainer will use the course materials to excite one or more of our senses, thus aiding the learning experience.

Cameo

In chapter 1 I asked you to visualize a cube. You may have found this difficult because visualization is not your main channel for recall. You may feel or hear things instead. I have two friends who are accomplished musicians. One is an organist, double-bass player and conductor, whilst the other is a pianist. The former can only play if he has the score, whilst the other can play for an hour without one. The former 'sees' the music whilst the latter 'hears' the music. When learning a new piece the pianist, even though he can read music, will usually listen to it three times on a tape or CD and then start to play it. One way is not better than the other, it is just different.

Let us explore some of the materials which are available to help excite those channels of communication.

VISUAL AIDS

A picture is worth 1000 words.

Other examples of commonly used visual training aids are: flipchart, white/blackboard, pin board, overhead projector and pictures/charts.

Flipcharts
Advantages

- Can be prepared in advance.
- No power supply needed.

Cameo

In the mid-1980s the international computer company Digital Equipment Corporation wished to provide its customers with business and IT strategy consultancy services. This was to be a big change in direction for the company because until then most of the consultancy offered was of a purely technical nature with technical expert talking to technical expert. This style of consultancy was not appropriate when working with senior managers and company directors while they explored their business strategy. The solution, devised by John Geesink, Bonnie Sontag and Charles Revkin from Digital's Geneva-based management consultancy group, was to develop a highly participative series of strategy workshops based on map building. The consultancy service was called TOP Mapping™. The workshop began with an explanation of the use of maps followed by a consultant providing some training in map building and the use of symbols, e.g. a swamp representing lost information. The business executives were put into teams of three and built maps of how they saw their organization. These highly visual representations of the organization were then used as presentation aids between the teams. The delegates gained a much deeper insight into the issues and developed a common understanding of the organization. At a later stage in the workshop series they also made a map of their future vision. Executives generally found this simple and visual approach very powerful in helping to develop their strategy.*

* The original TOP Mapping consultancy service has now evolved into SEE Mapping™ which is available through Atticus Ltd.

- Easy to use and write on.
- Able to use colour.
- Easy for students to see.
- Usually easy to obtain.
- Easy to refer back to earlier sheets.

Disadvantages

- Large and cumbersome when transported.
- Can look messy.
- Short life before looking dog-eared/untidy.
- Masking difficult.
- Expensive if professionally prepared.

In general flipcharts are good for spontaneous explanations or data capture, big visual pictures and for small group work – discussions and presentations. If possible always have one or two available, even if you do not plan to use them.

Figure 5.1 demonstrates some tips on using a flipchart.

1. If possible use perforated sheets for easy tearing, otherwise score top with a ruler and cut in about 10mm each side to ensure a smooth tear.
2. For quick access 'tab' the sections.
3. Use the top corner to write any notes about the chart. Write small so that no one notices but you.
4. Lightly pencil outlines in advance, e.g. a flow chart you are going to develop, if you are not sure how much space you will need.
5. Cut off corners of preceding sheets if you need quick access to a particular page.

Further tips:

- Always prepare flipcharts in advance of the session.
- Use big lettering.
- Leave lots of space between points – a maximum of 7 points/lines to a sheet.
- Use pictures and cartoons to add interest.
- Face the audience whilst writing on the flipchart.

Whiteboards (the blackboard replacement)
Whiteboards have tended to replace the blackboard as a means of visual aid. Blackboards can remind some trainees of schooldays. Many training rooms have whiteboards in place; sometimes complete walls are devoted to them.

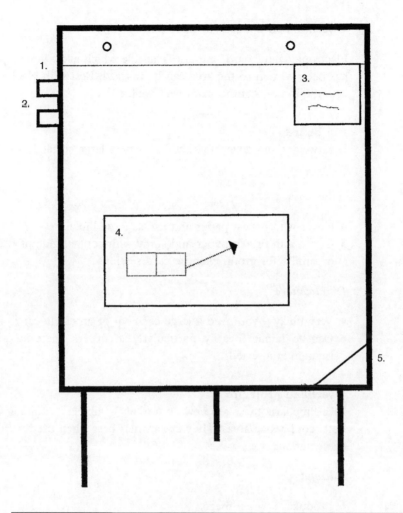

Figure 5.1 How to use a flipchart

Advantages

- Useful for 'note pad' work.
- Often metal backed which allows the use of magnetic disks to display prepared flipchart paper.
- Can use colour.
- Can be used for Post-Its™ in brainstorming-type exercises.

Disadvantages

- Needs special pens.
- Limited space and once full they have to be erased before additional comments can be added.

- Vertical and not easy to write on.

Electronic whiteboards are also available which allow you to print off what has been written so the area can be re-used. Best with black pens, as some colours do not seem to print very well.

Pin board
Lightweight and collapsible they provide a large surface area on which to work.

Advantages

- Cover with brown paper and use as large flipchart.
- Cover with brown paper and spray with contact glue or use BluTak™ or similar for group exercise card sessions.

Disadvantages

- Very bulky – you need a large car boot or an estate car to move it.
- Can be damaged easily, particularly at corners where the pins are frequently inserted.

Overhead projector
Like flipcharts these are now commonly available in training rooms and hotel conference areas. They are at their best when used with a prepared presentation.

Advantages

- Produces a large image.
- Overheads easily carried.
- Can be used with PC plasma tablets.
- Masking easy.
- Notes can be written in margins.

Disadvantages

- Needs electricity.
- Needs a screen or suitable wall.
- Can be noisy.
- Difficult to write on – requires practice.
- Bulbs can blow – provide a spare.

The smartest way to produce professional overheads is to use your PC; there is a wide selection of presentation and drawing software available.

Remember to obtain the correct acetates for either a laserprinter/
photocopier or inkjet printer. You can use images and/or colour to brighten
up your overhead as many of these packages come with clipart. My top
ten rules for preparing successful overheads are:

1. Keep overheads simple.
2. Be concise.
3. Use only one idea/topic per displayed overhead.
4. Use masking or follow-on overheads to develop an idea.
5. Use graphics and cartoons to help illustrate/reinforce a point.
6. Use colour to add interest or emphasis.
7. Legibility depends on the letter size, thickness, spacing and distance
   from the screen. Use 5mm-high letters for up to 10 metres from the
   screen, 10mm-high letters for 10–15 metres and 15mm-high for
   15–20 metres' distance.
8. Keep to a maximum of seven lines per overhead.
9. Keep to a maximum of seven words per line.
10. Do not use reproduced typed textbook pages or reports – they break
    all the legibility rules.

Before the event position the OHP and screen so that everybody can see it
clearly (sit in the students' seats to check it out). Decide where you are
going to stand when you make the presentation and where you will locate
your overheads. Check that you can turn off the lights and close any
blinds easily and finally make sure you have a spare bulb with you.

Pictures, charts and maps
Pictures, charts and maps can add that extra dimension to a presentation.
The earlier cameo examined the power of maps and in the same way
pictures can make powerful illustrations of a point and charts are excellent
for taking students through the logic of a process. The excellent trainer has
a knack of spotting pictures etc. that will enhance a presentation. You
could gather together a library of interesting illustrations that might be of
use in the future.

HEARING AND VISUAL AIDS

• Video – hearing, visual and, possibly, emotional.
• Tape recording – hearing.

The following examples encompass senses other than the solely visual.
Video is an extremely powerful medium but the tape recorder can also
add a new dimension to your presentation. You only need to look at old
newsreel footage of politicians and statesmen to see how they used music

to excite their audience before they began their oratory. But examples are not just confined to the archives. Many of today's leaders, captains of industry, entertainers and sportsmen still use music before they begin, for whilst it uses the hearing channel music can influence the emotions.

Video
Video is now used extensively in training either as part of a session's input or as a feedback device.

As an input aid video can provide powerful reinforcement to any session. It can add sound, movement, colour and humour and has the added bonus that it can be paused and/or rerun to explore points as they arise. You can use video as the basis for discussion. For example, ask: 'What happens next?' or 'What would you have done in that situation?'

The main drawback to its use is cost. Prices range from £75 to more than £900, and consequently it will have to be used a number of times to justify the initial investment. This may seem cheap when compared to having a video made by a professional film company, which will cost considerably more and also requires a significant input of management time to ensure you get what you want.

The first golden rule for using video as a presentation is that you should see it in its entirety prior to the event to check that it does deliver the required message no matter how many famous and/or funny people it has in the cast. Do not rely on the sleeve notes to help you decide on how to use it. Watch it, and make detailed notes so you can stop it in the correct place and ask pertinent questions.

As a feedback aid video is probably the best teacher when used in interpersonal skills training. It is much more powerful than an observer's comments because the person is able to see their own behaviour. Video feedback incorporated into coaching sessions will enable the students to see how their performance changes.

The second golden rule is to ensure that everybody understands how the medium will be used in the training and that, unless agreed by the students to the contrary, the tape will be wiped clean at the end of the session. I knew of one trainer who failed to contract with the students at the start of a course concerning the use of video. When the camera appeared the course came to an abrupt halt. A student who had some experience of political repression objected on the grounds that the video might be seen by persons outside of the course and out of context. It took a long time to allay his fears and many caveats were introduced to reassure him.

Tape recording

Tape recorders are an excellent training aid. They can provide:

- appropriate background, introductory or closing music
- a sound track to a slide presentation
- examples to illustrate a presentation point
- feedback by using one of our senses, not two as with video (e.g. role plays, presentations).

The golden rule for tape recording is always leave a short space between recorded items. You then only need to press the 'pause' button at the end of each item and then release it to hear the next one. In the same way as using video, you should practice with the tape recorder a few times before introducing it into the session and listen to any pre-recorded material in its entirety before you use it.

FEELING AIDS

Models and props

Whilst models may be considered a visual aid – for example, a scale model of a building or car – they have been included with feeling aids because very often they can also be picked up. Props on the other hand is a catch-all term for many aids which affect all the senses but in particular

Cameo

It was a warm afternoon and the trainer needed to introduce an energizer to liven up the group. As she looked around the training room her eyes spied a fruit bowl with a dozen small oranges in it that had been left by the hotel staff. Quickly she passed the bowl round and each person took an orange. They were then told to examine their orange closely and really get to know it, by its smell, its texture, its colour and to also observe any blemishes or marks. She then asked the group members to find a partner and take it in turns to describe their orange to each other. After this exercise she collected up the oranges and put them back in the bowl in the middle of the group. The group was then asked to find THEIR own personal orange. Everybody found his or her orange.

feeling. I keep a small bag of unusual items like a piece of sponge, a jar top, a shoehorn from a Christmas cracker, a short length of chain etc. and their use has frequently livened up an exercise or presentation.

Always have an emergency facilitation kit with you. A pack of Post-Its™, some coloured marker pens and adhesive tape are excellent for running unexpected workshops. You never know when you will need them. A consultant I know used them to good effect on a table top in the dining car of the London (Euston) to Manchester train when she facilitated an impromptu meeting of business executives who were at her table.

Handouts and other materials

Participants cannot be expected to simply sit and listen. They need to participate actively and remember what has happened during the event. The materials you issue to the students can help to achieve this. In most instances these materials will be handouts, based on the training event and distributed before, during or after each session.

The notes need not reproduce exactly what you intend to say and may just be copies of your overheads which can be annotated during the session as and when people remember what they have heard or seen. Whether the handouts are a full transcript of events, outline notes or copies of slides/overheads, they must be attractive, logical and memorable. Handouts contained in ring binders with dividers and/or index and contents pages will make them accessible and will provide you with some flexibility around when you issue them to the students. Do not underestimate how long it takes to prepare handouts or how long the reprographic department or printers take to copy and bind them. My rule of thumb is to have all the handouts completed three weeks before a one-week training event. This allows plenty of time for their reproduction. This apparent long lead-time is based on many bitter experiences when my materials have been poorly printed, incorrectly collated and even lost. Having to apologize at the beginning of an event for the lack of handout material is not an auspicious way to start.

Other participant material requirements, like pencils, paper, handbooks and tools etc., should be identified during the design phase and requisitioned in plenty of time for the event. Make a checklist of all the materials you require for the event, tick them off when they are ordered and again when you receive them, and you will avoid sleepless nights and panic as the event approaches. You do not need that kind of stress as you prepare yourself for launching the event. An example checklist is included in the Compendium.

The evening before

Although this section is entitled 'The evening before' it is just as appropriate at any time before the event and even possibly during one. You have arrived at the venue and checked in. Now start mentally preparing yourself and checking that nothing has been left to chance. Take your time, particularly if you have been travelling for a few hours. If possible take a shower and change your clothes; this will help move yourself from travelling mode to teaching mode. Begin by walking around the venue to get a 'feel' for the location and introduce yourself to the venue management. Order a coffee and relax, drinking it slowly in a public area and watch what is going on around you.

Having spent a short time relaxing, meet with the venue management to confirm meal and break arrangements, the rooms you will be using during the event and any special requirements. Proceed to your training room. Start by checking that all the materials have been delivered and work. If not, chase whoever is responsible for logistics and/or the venue management. Next check that any breakout/syndicate rooms are correctly set up. Then return to the main room and review the layout, ensuring that all the students can see the presentations and interact with each other. Sit in each chair. Finally, move to where you will be presenting, visualize the room full of students and imagine you are opening the first session. Quietly take yourself through those first few opening minutes and repeat it until you feel comfortable in your own mind.

If there are co-trainers you will also need to discuss the event so that they understand their roles. Depending on their experience you may also wish to conduct some final rehearsals rather than just use visualization. Relax and eat together to help team bonding. If you have worked together many times before you will probably have developed some rituals to help re-establish the bonds. If possible, have an early night – you will need lots of energy for the next few days.

6 DURING THE EVENT

The design, preparation and planning are over. It is now time to meet the delegates who, being human, add that unpredictable element into the training equation. It all adds to the buzz of running the event.

Leading the event

You can lead a horse to water but you cannot make it drink.

Proverb

The start will often set the tone for the whole event. Not only are the delegates likely to be new to you they may well be new to each other. The golden rules for establishing a good basis are first, be enthusiastic and, second, encourage interaction as soon as possible. Use an 'ice breaker' exercise to help you, and keep your eyes and ears open to spot both the quiet and the over keen ones. Once the introductions are completed, outline the event's purpose, timetable and any associated logistics. Whilst it may appear rather mundane, this housekeeping session is important because it allows you to lay down the ground rules which will establish a smooth-running event.

The art and science of communication

Before examining the skills it is also worth examining the process of communication (see Figure 6.1).

The sender is transmitting information or ideas and the receiver needs to understand the message and its meaning. There are many ways in which the message's meaning and understanding can be lost.

- Coding the message. The 'language' that you use to convey the message. It may be verbal or non-verbal like the visual aids or overheads that are used during the presentation.

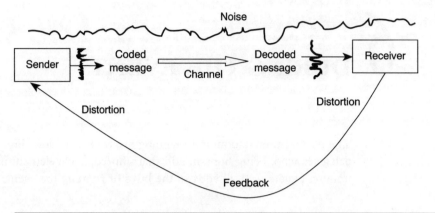

Figure 6.1 The communication process

- The medium for the message.   In a presentation the primary medium will be the spoken word. It can also be a computer or video if these are being used in support of the presentation. Choosing the most appropriate medium to deliver the message is vital.
- Distortion.   The way in which the meaning of the message is lost. For example, if the language is inappropriate to the audience or contains jargon then the receiver may be unable to decode it or will decode it incorrectly. The audience may also decode incorrectly because of prejudice, preconceived ideas or because the presenter's body language or use of voice is inconsistent with what is being said. Many people only hear what they expect to or want to hear.
- Noise.   The distractions or interference in the environment in which the communication is taking place. For example, physical noise like passing traffic, or psychological noise like tiredness or frustration, or cultural noise if delegates are drawn from a number of countries.

All these breakdowns in communication can result in the information you are giving not being correctly received. This is neatly summed up by a saying attributed to ex-President Richard Nixon: 'I know that you understand what you think I said, but I am not sure you realize that what you heard is not what I meant'. Which clearly demonstrates the need for the last element of communication, feedback. Feedback is important because you can test both the students' understanding and reaction to the information you have given. The skilled presenter will observe feedback at two levels:

- The audience will give feedback with their body language and general interest and interaction with the presenter.

Cameo

A remote hotel in East Anglia had been booked for a day of client presentations. All had gone well until lunchtime but as I rose to my feet to give a talk on management consulting the whole hotel shook as a jet roared overhead. I waited until it had passed and commenced again, only to be drowned out a second time. This same thing happened again and again so I stopped the presentation, suggested we had a five-minute break and asked the organizer to find out from reception what was the cause. The adjournment became permanent when it was discovered that the hotel was close to the flight path of a USAF base and that a 72-hour NATO exercise had just begun. The organizer had wondered why the conference rates had been so reasonable!

- The presenter will introduce activities that will 'test' the audience's understanding of the subject matter. It may take the form of questions, formally during the session or informally over a beer, or an exercise that employs the ideas given during the presentation.

Having obtained feedback the presenter can decide what action, if any, needs to be taken to help get the message across.

Student listening and attention span

Another important element of communication is the student's ability to listen actively during the presentation. Research indicates that input sessions should be kept to a maximum of forty minutes. Longer presentations could overload the student. During a single media presentation students are more likely to be attentive at the start, their minds will then wander off during the middle section and they will return to the subject towards the end. It is a challenge for all trainers to employ strategies which help the students to receive all the information being presented.

Presentation rules

1. Check your dress before starting. Undone zips, shirts or blouses hanging out and crooked ties can easily become the focus of the student's attention rather than your words.

Cameo

A very nervous trainer was holding an extendable pointer whilst giving a presentation. At the start of the presentation the pointer was at its minimum length, but as she talked she fiddled with the pointer and over a period of some five minutes slowly extended it to its maximum. It then magically became a conductor's baton as she waved it around in time to some silent orchestra. The whole audience became transfixed by the pointer and hardly heard a word she was saying to them.

2. Begin with a moment's silence and make eye contact with all the students.
3. During the silence take three deep breaths before you start speaking.
4. Start with a bang.
5. Tell them how they will benefit from listening to the presentation, i.e. what is in it for them.
6. Tell them what you are going to tell them, tell them, and tell them what you have told them.
7. Encourage some audience participation early on in the session.
8. Use your voice to maintain interest by speaking:
   • clearly and loudly so that everybody can hear
   • with a varied tone and pitch
   • at different speeds to excite or emphasise.
9. Continue eye contact with participants throughout the session. It gives them the impression that you are speaking to individuals personally which helps to hold their attention.
10. Avoid mannerisms like playing with props, jangling loose change in your pocket or saying 'OK', 'You know' or some similar phrase.
11. End with a bang.
12. Stick to the schedule.

Leading a discussion

Presentation skills do not stop at delivery. The discussion that surrounds the presentation is another important element in a training event. Students will often learn a great deal from interaction and trainers must be able to initiate and maintain group discussions. There are a number of ways that the trainer can facilitate this process.

Normally you would lead the discussion with a question, closed or open. A closed question has a set answer: 'What colour was his hair?' An open question allows the respondent to be more expansive: 'What do you think about . . .?' or 'How do you feel about . . .?' As the trainer you should encourage or lubricate the responses. The encouragement can be both verbal and non-verbal.

Verbal

- 'Tell me more about . . .'
- 'I see.'
- 'Go on'.
- 'Ah, ah.'

Non-verbal

- Nodding.
- Leaning forward.
- Maintaining eye contact.
- Using your hand to draw out like a traffic policeman.

The 'Learning in groups' section of this book (Chapter 2, p. 20) briefly explored some of the group dynamics which might come into play during a training session. Be sensitive to these dynamics when leading a discussion and recognize when to 'push' the group and when to take a 'hands off' approach. You will probably do more pushing during the early phases of a group's development and take your 'hands off' once the group is performing. The ability to lead a group when it is attempting to resolve a complex and ambiguous problem is a notable skill that the excellent trainer will have developed over many years.

Dealing with difficult situations

This section examines those difficult situations which are introduced by the participants. Situations brought about by management, the venue and logistics in general, are examined elsewhere at appropriate points in the book. The important point to remember is the application of Murphy's Law – 'If it can go wrong, it will' – but more spectacularly than you ever imagined. Careful planning can reduce the likelihood of many of these potential difficult situations. By designing an excellent course which meets the organization's needs and by fully preparing the participants and their managers for the event you will also diminish the risk of meeting difficult

Cameo

My colleague and I had been running a consulting skills course for a number of years, an important element of which was communication skills. Within this element was a session on 'The games people play'. To illustrate the theory my colleague and I acted out a number of popular 'office' games which were followed by group discussion. On one occasion after this session a female member of the group, who had been fully engaged in the course, became very quiet. At the next break my colleague enquired whether there was a problem and discovered that one of the games we had demonstrated was precisely what had happened to her a few years earlier, but she had not realized it was a 'game'. Seeing the whole event played out in front of her including the 'pay off' had brought back all the emotions she had experienced at the time. Fortunately my colleague, a trained counsellor, was able to help her and by the next day she returned to her old, but also wiser, self.

participants. However, human beings are interesting and unpredictable material, with a variety of personal experiences which will influence their behaviour during the training event. Individuals can react quite unexpectedly to a session and may need attention to help them and the rest of the group learn.

The most common forms of behaviour that you might encounter when leading a training event are now examined.

THE KNOW-IT-ALL

There will usually be one or two very talkative people who wish to 'show off' their knowledge. Sometimes they know little but just like to chatter (the empty vessel). These types need little encouragement to contribute.

- When asking a question make eye contact elsewhere to allow other members of the group an opportunity to become involved.
- If a know-it-all is talking at length, wait for a pause, briefly summarize, refocus and move on.
- Ask a tough question to slow them down.

Variants

- Rambling talkers – stop with a question.
- Red herrings – surface the red herring and return to the subject.

THE MOANER

'Ain't it awful' is the pet phrase of the moaner. It may be the course, the organization he/she works in, or life in general. This state of mind can become infectious if there are a number of people from the same organization or background so you will need to deal promptly with this behaviour.

If the moans are about the course ask the moaner to specify the issues as openly and honestly as possible. An earlier cameo showed that in the final reckoning it might be best if they leave the course, but that should be seen as the last resort.

If it is just one moaner peer pressure will often resolve the situation.

Where the group as a whole has serious concerns about its organization it is often best to introduce a short sharp session to get it off their chest. You are unlikely to make much progress until they have left that baggage behind.

THE ARGUER

An arguer will get satisfaction from challenging you – maybe he just enjoys an argument, or he could be aggressive by nature.

- Either way, stay calm. Do not get upset or drawn into a protracted confrontation or stand off.
- When a correct statement is made, express agreement.
- When an incorrect statement is made, open up the discussion to the group for a correction. 'What do the rest of you think?'

THE WHISPERER

There are a number of reasons and solutions for whispering:

- Boredom – encourage the whisperer's involvement.
- Someone does not understand and is having an explanation – implement a strategy to help understanding.
- Sitting with a friend or someone they would like to make friends with – request that small talk be reserved for breaks. Peer pressure can be employed in this instance.

The 'power of silence' will often stop whispering, especially if combined with eye contact. You must discover the reason for the whispering.

Cameo

During a course to a combined Austrian and German audience that was being delivered in English there was a great deal of whispering amongst most of the Austrian and a couple of the German delegates and every so often one of the Germans would ask a question. During a break I enquired if there was a problem. It transpired that whilst the Austrians were able to understand what I was saying, they found it difficult to formulate questions because they were translating what I said into German, thinking about it in German, formulating a question in German and translating it into English. By the time they had formulated the question the discussion had moved on and the point was lost. So instead they kept a dialogue going with Germans who had a better (faster) command of the English language. Not a very satisfactory arrangement.

As we explored the problem it became apparent that the greatest difficulty was translating their question into English. The solution for them was not to spend time trying to translate but to ask any questions in German. Whilst I did not understand the question, it immediately told me to stop presenting. Then, as a group we had fun translating it into English so that I could answer. It took a little longer but it bonded the group more strongly.

THE QUIET ONE

The most likely cause of quietness is that the student is either timid or bored. Body language and other behaviour should help you identify to which category they belong.

- Encourage the timid ones with easy questions and bolster their confidence.
- Involve the bored ones by letting them participate in exercises, plan a session or even given a presentation.

LOSS OF FOCUS

Any of the above situations can result in the group losing focus and the whole discussion or presentation may start to collapse. To bring the group back on line:

- Summarize and/or ask a closed question. Refer the group to an overhead or slide to refocus on the subject.

Cameo

> Jacky, a primary school teacher, was giving an English lesson to her class when a small frog hopped into the classroom. Not surprisingly the children were distracted by this unexpected visitor and were unable to concentrate on the lesson at hand. Instead of letting this incursion spoil the lesson she seized the moment and refocused the lesson around the frog. The children's work was wonderful, covering not only English, but also science, mathematics and art. It was pure serendipity.

LOSS OF ATTENTION / INTEREST

In the preface to my book *75 Ways to Liven Up Your Training* I describe an incident where the combination of lunch and hot weather made it impossible for the students to concentrate. When such a crisis point occurs be flexible and move away from the original design – in the incident described I organized a game instead of the planned presentation. Always prepare something to introduce at short notice when you need to change the pace and style of the event. A five- or ten-minute exercise will not only liven up the delegates, but will also buy you time should you need to do a quick session redesign. Think of your course design as the plan for a military campaign. Events happen during battles that were not anticipated at the planning stage. Successful commanders have the flexibility to respond and turn the unexpected to their advantage.

MORE GOLDEN RULES

The golden rules for handling any difficult training situation are:

- Stay calm.
- Never argue, belittle or resort to sarcasm.
- Find out what the real problem is.
- Show that you understand the problem.
- State your position.
- If necessary, point out benefits to be gained by a change in behaviour and, if that fails, the consequences of not changing.
- Check frequently that you are understanding the problem.
- Use the group to help resolve it.
- Remember the power of silence.

7 CLOSING THE EVENT – AND BEYOND

A fool says, I can't; a wise man says I'll try.
Proverb

Training does not end as the last delegate leaves. It is often only the start and the trainer can play an important role in guaranteeing further learning.

Just as the opening session sets the tone for the whole event the closing session provides the foundations on which the students' future learning will be based. The closing session should comprise three elements:

- a reflection and feedback of the event
- an opportunity for students to plan their next steps in the learning process
- the start of disengagement, including the chance to say farewells and prepare for re-entry into home and business life.

The amount of time spent on the third element will depend on the length of the course. A half-day event is unlikely to include significant disengagement, whereas a one-week course that has involved team working will need to reserve some quality time for that process.

Reflection and feedback

The closing session will be you, the trainer, 'telling them what you've told them', coupled with them, the trainees, telling you what they thought of the experience. A minimalist approach is to run through the agenda restating the important message of each session. This approach works well for the half- or one-day event.

For longer events there should be a full-scale recap of each day's activities with an end-of-course review on the last day. This exercise also provides an opportunity for student feedback about the training. Feedback is most important if your training is to be both appropriate and responsive to an organization's needs. By running the course properly and developing a good relationship with your students there should be no major surprises in the feedback.

Before you run the feedback session think about your reaction to the event:

- Which sessions worked well, and why?
- Which sessions did not work as well as you had hoped, and why not?
- Were there any surprises?
- Any serendipity?
- What were the students like?
- What would you change, and why?

Finally record your general reaction to the event.

In addition to feedback/appraisal forms, a semiformal framework to prompt discussion at the end of the event will often draw out a richness and depth of response that a feedback form rarely achieves. Your own thoughts about the event may provide a good lead in the discussion. I tend to use a combination of formal and informal approaches. (For an example of a feedback/appraisal form, see the Compendium).

The student feedback elicited at the review stage of the training event is of great value.

- It gives their immediate reactions.
- It tests the amount of learning which has taken place.
- It provides suggestions for future events.
- It can be used as your basis for a summary report back to management.

If you are running a series of events, this feedback will also help you to modify future sessions so that they meet the students' needs more closely. But remember, you do not have to change. Consider the feedback carefully and decide what action, if any, you wish to take. Probably of greater importance will be the training evaluation you undertake three to six months after the event, when you test the impact of the training on both the individual and the organization.

Throughout the event watch out for interesting, amusing or unusual occurrences, particularly those which can be associated with specific activities. It will add interest and make the review more memorable when

Cameo

One of my courses included a tower-building exercise. A key test for the tower was its ability to support 20 kilograms. One team was so confident with their construction that instead of the 20 kilogram weight they elected to use a petite member of their group for the test. She weighed about 40 kilograms and two male team members gently lifted her onto the 'tower' which, although it buckled, supported her for the required 30 seconds. Everybody cheered. At the end-of-course review I arranged for a cartoon to be drawn of her balancing precariously, which was presented to her when we recalled that session. Some years later I met a member of the rival team who, even though they had not 'won', recalled the session fondly and, more importantly, also remembered why the rival group's construction had been so much more successful.

you recount these occurrences. Always use positive experiences which support your review.

Planning future learning

Chapter 5 of the book emphasized the importance of preparing the delegate and his/her manager so that they derive maximum benefit from the event, and also noted that attending a training course was not an end in itself but just one element of a trainee's development. In order to ensure their future development the trainer should use the closing session to guide students in their next steps. If the students have been working together in small teams during the event it is beneficial to group them into those same teams so that they help each other to develop their learning plans. The 'Action Aides' exercise from *75 Ways to Liven Up Your Training* (see Compendium) is one method to develop student plans and discuss their proposals within the group. Alternatively students could form themselves into an action learning group, as outlined earlier in this book. The important element is that the group should both support and challenge each member's learning action plan. This is explored more fully in 'Beyond the event' later in this chapter.

Disengagement

Disengagement is a vital element of the closing-off process – ignore it at your peril. Where trainees have been working in small groups, allow them

Cameo

In the late 1970s I attended a five-week executive development course. It was an extremely intensive course with significant amounts of team working and tight deadlines. This resulted in a very close camaraderie to the extent that some UK members did not go home at weekends, and any that did rushed back on Sunday afternoon. At the end of the course there was a closing session, but it did not include disengagement. I vividly remember everybody sitting together for our last lunch before we returned home. It was held in virtual silence and when we finished our meal nobody moved for many minutes. Finally Jan, a Dutchman who had a plane to catch, stood and said his farewells. At that point everybody burst into tears and started hugging each other. It was all very emotional and rushed. On reflection, even though many years have passed, I still feel cheated by not partaking in a proper 'closing-off'.

some time to say their group farewells before your main closing-off session. (The closing section of *75 Ways to Liven Up Your Training* contains a number of exercises for both small and large group sessions.)

Always remind delegates to:

- Take some time to say your farewells.
- Drive carefully, particularly if you have not driven for a few days.
- Re-enter 'home' sensitively, remembering that your spouse/partner/ parent/friend may also have been doing things while you have been away which they wish to share.
- Keep in touch.

Finally, as the leader or co-trainer, give yourself time to say your farewells to the students and other trainers. When you leave, remember what you said to the delegates about driving carefully and re-entry to home life. Try to avoid dwelling on the course as you motor home.

Beyond the event

We've only just begun . . .
The Carpenters

As noted earlier, training does not stop at the end of the course. In fact the real development normally starts after the training event, but as the course trainer you may not be personally involved any further.

Organizations and their type of training vary and your influence may not be particularly great once the students are away from the classroom.

Learning-focused organizations will promote continuing personal development and on-the-job training, with support from coaches, mentors and action learning groups, and your training event will provide just one element of a person's development. If you know that these approaches are not employed within the organization, you should explain how recall will significantly reduce over a few days and you should encourage the students to use their new skills, knowledge or techniques as early as possible in their work situation. You could suggest that the group form themselves into a learning network where they can provide support for each other and where you would be available as a resource to the group, possibly as a facilitator. Of course, this would depend on your own availability, enthusiasm and the organizational politics. Alternatively, each student could return to their workplace with a 'Next steps' form or action plan (see Compendium) which is used as the basis of student and manager debriefing discussions. Either method should remind managers of any commitments they gave during the pre-course briefing session.

EVALUATION

At the beginning of this chapter I discussed the end-of-course feedback process which provides you, the trainer, with an instant snapshot of students' reaction and what they felt they learnt. This immediate feedback is useful to you as a guide to the success of the event, but of greater value is an understanding of how it affected both the individual and his/her organization's performance. Typically you should wait three to six months, perhaps longer, to judge the event's true impact. Even then the result may be obscured by other changes that have taken place, but some data is better than no data. Most importantly, anything gleaned at this juncture should form the basis of reports to management. The reports should assess the effectiveness of the training and make recommendations for future events and/or changes to current learning practices within the organization.

OWN DEVELOPMENT

Training is an exciting and challenging activity. When you are involved in the daily hurly-burly of training it is all too easy to forget about your own development. Take the opportunity, when you review the course feedback and evaluations, to reflect on your own training needs. Is there a common theme emerging that indicates a development need? Are there additional skills you would like to acquire that will help you to become/remain an excellent trainer? Use your co-trainers, students and manager as a feedback resource to help reduce the 'Johari' blind and private areas and thereby release more of your locked potential. By adopting such an approach you will become a more effective trainer and, it is hoped, an *excellent* trainer.

Keep away from people who try to belittle your ambitions. Small people always do that, but the really great make you feel that you, too, can become great.
Mark Twain

A COMPENDIUM OF FORMS AND DOCUMENTS

Drawn by Simon Jarvis

Introduction

This Compendium contains examples of the documentation used during the training need identification and the design, development and delivery of a training event. It is unlikely that they will meet all your needs precisely, rather you should use them as the basis of your own approach to training. The majority of documents are examples of forms that could be used at specific times within the training cycle. The Course Development document provides some illustrative pointers to a number of the key stages during a training event's design and development.

The Radiocommunications Agency has kindly allowed me to use a number of its forms as examples. These forms are Crown Copyright.

Personal development

PERSONAL ACHIEVEMENT PLAN

The personal achievement plan is a working document used by jobholders and their line managers. It should set out both job-related and personal development objectives. It should be kept up to date, the objectives covered in the plan indicating clear target dates for their achievement. The plan aims to help individuals relate their personal objectives to business objectives.

RESTRICTED - STAFF

See Staff Appraisal Guidance Notes, Section C.

PERSONAL ACHIEVEMENT

Name:

Management Unit:

Line Manager:

Planning Year:

Job Description / Title

Review dates for diaries:

Notes:

The Personal Achievement Plan is intended to be a working document to be used by job holders and their line managers. The plan should set out both job related and personal development objectives. It will need to be revised regularly: how often will depend on local circumstances. The SAR process requires **at least two review sessions** - one at the end of the cycle and another some time during the reporting year.

The objectives covered in the Plan should have clear target dates for their achievement. The outcome should be recorded, including comments on why specific objectives were not met. This information will be important in completing the SAR at the end of the year.

The Plan will help individuals to relate their personal and work objectives to Agency/Business Unit objectives, in with best practice promoted by Investors in People, and to the Agency training and development strategies.

PAP 1997

DWA 5565 CON 0144

PLANNING PERIOD

Relevant management unit/section objectives

Work objectives	Target dates
Personal/Development objectives	Target dates

FROM: *TO:*

Action and timing	Action taken/Outcomes
Action and timing	Action taken/Outcomes

Personal achievement plan – continued

PLANNING PERIOD_____FROM:_____TO:_____
Name:_____
Management unit:_____
Grade:_____

Training and Development Needs related to Work Objectives	Timing	Action Taken / Outcomes

Training and Development Needs related to Personal / Development Objectives	Timing	Action Taken / Outcomes

Personal achievement plan – concluded

STAFF APPRAISAL REPORT

The staff appraisal report is an example of an annual appraisal. It examines current performance as well as future requirements. The personal achievement plan is examined and updated during the appraisal process.

RESTRICTED - STAFF

STAFF APPRAISAL REPORT

You must guard against unfair discrimination

1.Job Holder's Personal Details

See Staff Appraisal Guidance Notes:
Section D.1.

Name: Staff Number:

Substantive Grade:

Present Management Unit:

Current Office Address: Telephone No:

Period of Report:

Time spent on Temporary Promotion or Substitution during the reporting
Period_____months

Reporting Officer: Countersigning Officer:

Use additional sheets for your comments if there is insufficient space in the form.
Return completed form to relevant Personnel Section by 31 May at the latest

For use in Personnel Section:
Date report received...

Clerical Check	On PERMIS/PARIS	Performance Pay Notes

2. Current Job.

See Staff Appraisal Guidance Notes:
Section D.2.

3. Achievements

See Staff Appraisal Guidance Notes:
Section D.3.

4. Personal Effectiveness

See Staff Appraisal Guidance Notes:
Section D.4.

5. Overall Assessment

See Staff Appraisal Guidance Notes:
Section D.5.

Give a rating for overall performance using the rating scale, which is covered in more detail in the Staff Appraisal Guidance Notes (section D.5).

Rating Scale

1	Outstanding.
2 + / 2	Performance above normal requirements.
3 + / 3	Performance met the normal requirements of the job.
4	Performance not up to the requirements of the job.
5	Unacceptable.

Rating

Designed by PER/PDU

Staff appraisal report – continued

6. Core Skills / Attributes

6.1. Management

See Staff Appraisal Guidance Notes: Section D.6.

6.1(a): Managing People

6.1(b): Managing Other Resources

6.2. Interpersonal Skills

6.3. Communication Skills

6.3(a): Written

6.3(b): Oral

6.4. Analytical Skills and Judgement

Designed by PER/PDU

Page 3

Staff appraisal report – continued

6.5. Commitment

7. Additional Locally Agreed Skills / Attributes

See Staff Appraisal Guidance Notes:
Section D.7.

8. Progression

See Staff Appraisal Guidance Notes:
Section D.8.

Staff appraisal report – continued

9. Comments by the Job Holder

See Staff Appraisal Guidance Notes:
Section D.9.

10. Comments by the Countersigning Officer

See Staff Appraisal Guidance Notes:
Section D.10.

11. Signatures

See Staff Appraisal Guidance Notes:
Section D.11.

Job Holder..date..

Reporting Officer..date..

Countersigning Officer..date..

Designed by PER/PDU

Page 5

Staff appraisal report – concluded

Course development

OVERVIEW

The following documentation will take you through the main stages of a training course. They are designed to provide you with a sense of how a course develops together with some examples of forms etc. that might be employed. They are, as the saying goes, 'for the guidance of the wise and the adherence of the foolish'. Use them to aid your own approach to course development, for I doubt if you will find my 'shoes' entirely comfortable!

Note: Whilst they are primarily based on external training, the steps are the same for internal trainers. It is easy for an internal trainer, in an attempt to save time and money, to make assumptions and not properly document activities. You take short cuts or ignore them at your peril.

OUTLINE REQUIREMENTS

The following example is an extract from an outline requirement specification prepared by the training sponsor and sent to potential training providers. Being an outline it is necessary for the training provider to meet the sponsor in order to better understand the nature of the requirements and the most important areas.

Requirement for trainer to assist delivery of licence training procedures

Background

1. An internal audit report on licensing recommended the issue of manuals in a quality format to cover the use of the X computer system and policy procedures to be followed by staff within local offices and headquarters. Following the recent issue and circulation of these manuals to staff there is need to provide training based on material contained in the newly issued X Reference Manual and the Y Policy and Procedures Manual.

2. X is a .... The system is used by staff ranging from basic administrative skills to graduate engineers. The system has undergone a series of changes designed to improve performance, user friendliness and capability which has resulted in the requirement to update the system user manual.

3. Policy and procedures surrounding the issue of licences has been contained in a number of separate source documents which were in need of updating and rewriting.

4. The training of new staff in licence policy and procedures, through the use of the X system, now has to be undertaken in order that staff are able to issue licences of consistently good quality. Some preliminary training has recently been produced and delivered by A. The main components of this training have been identified as:

   - Training for administrative staff in headquarters and local offices in the best practice associated with the issue of licences, drawing on established policies and procedures and underpinning the supplementary training in the use of the X system.
   - Training to be carried out at three centres, beginning .... and ending ....
   - Each training event to last a total of two days, for a maximum of 12 people.
   - Training will be focused on delivery of services directly related to the business processes surrounding the issue of licences.

5. External ....

Specification

6. Provision of consultancy service from organizations with experience in the design and delivery of training with an IT background, to support the issue of licences. The external resource will need to understand quickly the main business processes involved; the interface between the A and local offices.

7. Phases within the project will encompass: design the training event; produce training materials for training staff and trainees; finalize logistics and invite trainees; finalize and deliver materials and stage 'rehearsal'; stage first event by ....

PROPOSAL AND PROJECT PLAN

Having read the requirements and met the training sponsor you can now develop an outline plan. The following example is an extract of a training proposal which would usually form the basis of the delivery. It is not unusual to have additional meetings to clarify points before the project commences.

There are five parts to the proposal. Parts 3 and 4 are outlined in detail so that you can appreciate the main phases of such a project.

Proposal to *Z* to support the delivery of licence training procedures

1. *Purpose of document*

2. *Introduction*

3. *Understanding of requirements*

From documentation and subsequent conversations we understand that the *Z*'s requirements are as follows:

- Design a two-day licence procedure training event combining operational procedures with use of the *X* system.
- Design all training and support materials to run a series of training events.
- Define in detail 'who does what, when and how' in a way that optimizes the effectiveness of the training – the needs to cover both the event and its administration.
- Support the rehearsals and attend the pilot of training and instigate any necessary refinements.
- Do ....

4. *Planned approach and methodology*

Phase 1: Assignment planning

Objectives

- Confirm terms of engagement, time scales and deliverables.
- Confirm planned approach and methodology, and identification and allocation of sponsor roles and resources.

Activities

- Meet sponsor to confirm objectives and identify resources.

Phase 2: Training needs analysis

Objectives

- Identify skills and knowledge of licensing administrator.
- Identify training event target audience.

Activities

- Review job descriptions and interview jobholders.
- Establish main 'can do's' associated with the role – use interviews or workshops.
- Identify skill and knowledge needs to perform the 'can do's' to acceptable standards.
- Develop training needs statement.
- Review with sponsor.

Phase 3: Procedures and systems review

Objectives

- Identify and document policy and procedure elements supporting the 'can do' statements.

Activities

- Review manuals.
- Chart main business processes.
- Document policies, procedures and systems supporting the business processes.
- Review with sponsor.

Phase 4: Course design

Objective

- Develop, using data already collected, course structure, materials and support needed.

Activities

- Develop training skeleton incorporating all exercises and activities to achieve 'can do's'.
- Estimate size of training modules.
- Check outline with sponsor.
- Check mix of learning approaches.
- Check that target audience interview findings are addressed.
- Draft training materials.
- Outline administration and logistics activities and time scales.
- Define reference material sources, subject matter experts and other support needed.
- Check training content fits local office working styles.
- Identify support needed from sponsor.

Phase 5: Training rehearsals and pilots

Objective

- Check that delivery will be to acceptable standard.

Activities

- Take individual trainers through materials – ensure they practise.
- Give inputs on training skills for trainers.
- Test course content.
- Attend and support pilot training and conduct reviews with trainees and trainers.
- Review with sponsor and agree changes.
- Amend training materials as agreed.

5. *Time scales and work plan*

This part will include phase start and end dates and general standards of work required.

NEEDS ANALYSIS INTERVIEW STRUCTURE

A number of interview structures were produced to suit different grades of local office staff. The objective was to elicit the critical 'can do's' for each particular role and identify what was common to, and different between, the roles. Administrative staff, operations managers, district managers and regional managers were interviewed. The following example was drawn up as a basis for interviewing the local office operations managers. Preparing a structure not only provides a framework for the interview, it also helps you to visualize the interview taking place. Again the structure is not meant to constrain the interview; it is offered here for guidance not adherence.

Operations Manager Example

Interview questions to identify areas for licence training.

Note: The questions are structured not solely to ask about 'can do's' or training needs. Procedural, system or organizational issues may also have a significant impact on the effective delivery of a licensing service. These issues are unlikely to be eliminated by training alone.

Interviewees are local office administrative staff, operations managers, district managers and regional managers. Expected interview time: approximately 45 minutes.

Operations manager – Reports to district manager

1. Introduction. Who, what, why, when, where and how is the project being undertaken?
2. Name and how long in job?
3. Briefly tell me about your job, particularly with respect to licensing (5 minutes). (Note: Check what starts the process and who follows on from the operations manager in the preparation of a licence?)
4. What training have you received to help you in this role? What has helped? What has not?
5. In what licensing areas do you think you would benefit from additional training? Why?
6. What do you think customers feel about the company and why?
7. Imagine that a customer has told you there are problems with his licence. What are they likely to be? How would they have been caused? How would you resolve them?
8. What do customers expect you to be able to do?
9. What are the critical 'can do's' for an administrator to undertake successful licensing work?
10. How do you ensure they 'can do'?
11. Is there anything in the licensing process undertaken by the administrators that you feel you should check?
12. What would you like to see covered in a training course for an administrator?
13. What are the critical 'can do's' for you to undertake successful licensing work?
14. What does the regional manager expect of you?
15. Is there anything the regional manager likes to personally check with a licence?
16. What licence problems give you the greatest headache? Why?
17. If you could wave a magic wand and change one or two things about the licensing process, what would they be? Why?
18. Where do you think you would benefit from additional training and why?

KEY POINTS FOR COURSE DESIGN

The interviews and other discussions led to the following requirements.

---

1. All administration staff and operations managers must be able to cover for each other.
2. Difference between them is management discretion and complexity of problem handling.
3. All need to understand the company policy towards licensing so that they can make an application and answer queries.
4. Thus the four 'can do's' are:
   - Can enter licence details for new applications and changes in accordance with company procedures.
   - Can answer customer enquiries about the status of their licence.
   - Can advise customers and their agents of the correct procedures for new applications or licence changes.
   - Can recognize technical enquiries and direct them to the appropriate person.
5. A fully competent administrative grade employee will have the following:

Knowledge
- Basic understanding of how the technology works.
- Understanding of why the company has to manage these resources.
- Understanding of two important aspects of the business, licensing and enforcement.
- Understanding of the total licensing process, including an appreciation of assignment.
- Knowledge of company procedures.
- Understanding of commonly used technical terms, e.g. type approval.
- Understanding of commonly used legal terms, e.g. partnership.
- Knowledge of local office/region organization.
- Knowledge of escalation procedures.

Skills

- Able to follow procedures and use X for both data entry and enquiry purposes, including cash handling, accounting, case registration, file tracking, case download and entering information for both existing and new licence applications.
- Able to handle customer enquiries sensitively yet firmly when necessary.
- Ably to apply policies appropriately.

Note: Job descriptions could be based on the above analysis, e.g. core skills and increasing levels of experience, management discretion and span of control. Training alone will not resolve all the issues raised. The licence application form needs to be redesigned.

COURSE OUTLINE

You will have identified a number of important training topics from the interviews. Think about these topics and decide in outline how the training might be delivered. Complete an outline form for each topic that identifies the learning objectives, the equipment needed, the subject matter and an estimate of the course duration. These forms will identify the resources needed for running the event, the training materials and outline timetable. There may be several iterations before you can start detailed planning and developing delivery materials.

Outline form

Course title	Licence training
Topic	Step-by-step explanation of the licence process
Equipment	Correctly completed licence application forms, procedure manuals, OHP, X test system, BARCO. Handout forms cross-referenced to procedures. Dummy incorrectly completed application forms. One PC between two trainees.
Learning objectives	Understand how the application form should be completed. The main policies and procedures that apply to the form. How the data should be entered into X. Appreciation of the technical side of building the licence.
Special considerations	Need to refer to appropriate policies. Test system must be up and working and able to cope with 10 simultaneous transactions.

Time	Items	Comments/Equipment in use
120 mins	Walk through a correctly completed application form	Test system, BARCO, manual, application forms, OHP.
	Issue application form handout showing procedure refs.	Handouts.
	Mention redesign of application form.	Be prepared for discussion on local processing.
	Issue dummy application forms.	
	Work in pairs to identify the errors and determine correct action.	Manual. Four incorrect application forms per pair. Have more than one error on some.
	Group discussion.	Ensure each pair is asked about an error.
	Open new account.	X test system etc.
	Cash handling and X entry. Over and under payment.	Test system. Including printer for pinks.
	Register case. Create a registered file.	Test system.
90 mins	Pairs practise with dummy application forms.	Issue some with errors and see if checked before data entry. Test system.
	Continue with similar exercises for updates, renewals and cancellations.	Some of the documentation should contain errors or be incomplete and need searches.
	Complete this session with a transfer that does not comply to policy and procedure.	
	Link with technical staff.	How can we make it easy for both?

TIMETABLE

Having completed the forms you can now produce the outline timetable. This should cover the topics, their approximate timings and who is responsible for its delivery. At this point course materials should be under production and there should be a high degree of confidence in proposed delivery time-scales. The following timetable was an early example; there were a number of minor changes to it during detailed design, rehearsals and pilots.

Outline timetable

Licence training – Overview

Day 1

10.00	Register	Kim Knight
10.15	Welcome	Dave Cowie
10.20	Introduction	Regional director
10.35	Housekeeping	Dave Cowie
	Objectives/Purpose	
	Agenda	
10.50	Learning objectives	Martin Orridge
	The Issue Wall	
11.10	BREAK	
11.25	Spectrum management	Peter Burton
11.45	Process overview	Dave Cowie
12.00	Application form presentation	Dave Cowie
	including TTO activities	
	and explanation of legal and technical terms	
	Technical video.	
13.00	LUNCH	
14.00	Licence process presentation continued	Dave Cowie
15.00	Paired work	Dave Cowie
15.30	BREAK	
15.45	RA1 Paired work continued	Dave Cowie
16.45	Check the cheque	Kim Knight
17.00	Anchor and close	Dave Cowie

Day 2

09.00	Welcome	Dave Cowie
	Recap and agenda	
09.15	Cash handling	Bob Willers
	and accounts	Kim Knight★
10.30	BREAK	
10.45	*X* data entry	Kim Knight
		Dave Cowie★
12.00	LUNCH	
13.00	Handling inquiries	Dave Cowie
	and customer care	Kim Knight★
		Martin Orridge
14.30	Local processing II	Dave Thomas
14.45	BREAK	
15.00	Issue board	Martin Orridge
15.45	Recap	Dave Cowie
16.00	Close	Dave Cowie

★ indicates system driver in support of presenter.

MATERIALS

Material requirements will also be identified on the course outline form. It is a good idea to identify at the earliest opportunity who will be responsible for their provision, as in the following example.

Licence training – materials required	
Material	*Supplied by*
Overhead masters	Atticus
Handout masters – copies of overheads	Atticus
Duplicated handouts	Client
Folders for trainees	Client
Flipcharts $\times$ 2	Client
10 Dry wipe markers – various colours	Client
$\frac{1}{2}$ Pack of Post-Its^{TM} per trainee	Client
Pen or pencil per trainee	Client
Pad of paper per trainee	Client
OHP	Client
Test database	Client
BARCO or similar projector	Client
12 Incorrectly completed licence application forms – variety of errors	Client, for use by trainees during event.
1 Dummy correctly completed application form	Client to Atticus a.s.a.p.
5 Blank application forms	Client to Atticus a.s.a.p.
1 PC per 2 trainees	Client
Copy of RAMPS and PBS manual	Client

VENUE LOGISTICS

If you are intending to run a training event 'off site' then you must check that the delivery location can address your needs. A 'good' venue will generally use a proforma, as in the following example used by the Wessex Hotel, Bournemouth. The proforma will have been completed during earlier discussions between the trainers and conference managers, usually at the time of booking the venue.

Hotel proforma
Sunday 24th–Friday 29th April 1994

Digital – Consulting Skills Course

Organiser:	Emma Goddard
	Digital Equipment Co. Ltd
	Digital Park
	Imperial Way
	Reading
	Berks
	RG2 0TE
Suites:	Main Room – Bryanston
	Synds – Dorset, 141, 142
Numbers	18 delegates + 3 Tutors
Room Layouts:	Bryanston
	U Shape × 18 with chairs only
	3 chairs at the top for the tutors
	4 tables at the side of the room for course materials
	Please provide chairs with arms
	Cordials and iced water to be on the tables
	Synds
	Boardroom × 5 in each
	Please note all conference rooms to be ready by 6.00pm on Sunday 24th
Equipment:	2 flipcharts and pens in Bryanston
	1 flipchart and pens in each synd.
	(5 in total)
	Please also provide extra pads
Note:	Their course equipment will be delivered on Sunday afternoon – pls store it securely in Bryanston

Timings:	Mon	Tues	Wed	Thu	Fri
Start:	10.00	9.00	9.00	9.00	9.00
Tea/Coffee/Danish:	10.00	10.30	10.30	10.30	10.30
Lunch:	1.00	1.00	1.00	1.00	1.00
Tea/Coffee/Doughnuts:	3.30	3.30	3.30	3.30	3.30
Dinner:	8.00	8.00	8.00	8.00	–
Finish:					6.00

Training application form

The training application form will be completed after a suitable development course has been identified. Normally the course should be referenced from the personal achievement plan. A full justification for the course should be apparent if the training need has not been identified.

RA2101 TRAINING APPLICATION FORM ☐

Please use this form for all training events. (For Civil Service College courses please complete form COL25 as well. For Job Related Foreign Language Training please add form DTI2117)

Please use separate form for each course

Section A Personal Details

Surname _____

Forenames
(BLOCK LETTERS) _____

Grade _____

Business Unit _____

Office Address _____

_____

Tel (incl GTN) _____

Section B Training Required

A) If you complete up to and including 3 and 4 only we will try to find a suitable course to meet your learning needs and contact you with a range of options before booking a course for you. B) If you know the course you require please complete the rest of section B.

1. **Subject Area:**
(Introduction to Word, Time Management, First Line Manager etc)

_____

2. **Competence Area:** _____

3. **Prefered Location:** _____

4. **When do you want the training:**

_____

5. **Name & Address of Provider:**
(If applying for a specific course,
(DETAILS INCLUDING COST MUST BE ATTACHED)

_____

_____

6. **Title of course:** _____

7. **Duration:** _____

8. **Preferred Dates:** _____

9. **Location of course:** _____

10. **Cost of course:** _____

11. Is this course part of your Personal Achievement Plan (P.A.P.) ?

Yes ☐ *Go to question 12.*

No ☐ *Go to question 13.*

12. What are your learning objectives ?
(TAKE FROM YOUR P.A.P.)

_____
_____
_____
_____
_____
_____
_____

13. Please specify how this additional training relates to (a) your P.A.P. objectives & (b) how it affects the training already identified on P.A.P)

_____
_____
_____
_____
_____
_____
_____
_____
_____
_____

Section C Adult Further Education

1) Subject _____

2) Name and address of college you propose to attend

_____

_____

_____

3) Qualification(s) sought

_____

_____

4) Academic year(s) _____

5) Course fee(s) £ _____

6) Examination fee £ _____
(if appropriate)

7) Cost of books £ _____
(if appropriate)

8) Have you tried to obtain this/these qualifications before?

Yes [ ]   No [ ]

If yes please give details _____

_____

_____

9) Timetable of subjects to be studied/classes to be attended

_____

_____

10) Present Qualifications
(with dates) _____

_____

_____

Note: You are obliged to inform RA6 if you do not complete the Adult Further Education applied for. RA6 reserve the right to recover from you all or part of any assistance provided in the event of withdrawal without good reason.

Section D Line Manager

How do you expect your member of staff's performance to be improved by this training?

_____

_____

_____

_____

_____

_____

_____

Signed _____

Name _____

Tel (inc GTN) _____

Date _____

Now pass this form to:

Section E Agency Training Manager

On confirmation of a place the cost of
£ _____ **should be charged against**

Expenditure Code _____

Ledger Heading _____

Date _____

Action _____

Signed _____

Name _____

Training application form – continued

To:

NAME   _____   Ref

Executive _____

Business Unit _____

Desk Address _____

From:

    _____

R6/TALU
Floor 10/Bay 26
Tel. No.

Date

RE : YOUR APPLICATION FOR TRAINING

COURSE   _____

DATE   _____

Further to your application for training I can now confirm that you have a place on the above event.

Further details and joining instructions will be forwarded nearer the time.

Please note that having been allocated a place you are committed to attend and withdrawal can only be considered in exceptional circumstances. Late withdrawal means that the Agency loses money. If you must withdraw, please contact

Unfortunately the date you have requested for this course is unavailable. The next available date will be:
_____Please let me know if you can attend this new date

Unfortunately your request for training has been denied for the following reasons:

_____

_____

_____

_____

If you have any queries about your application, please do not hesitate to contact me on the above number.

Training Coordinator

Training application form – concluded

Joining instructions

Joining instructions should be sent out in plenty of time, particularly if trainees are to make their own hotel arrangements.

To:

Don Bond
RA4/Bristol

From:

Kevin Delaney
Local Licensing Co-ordination Unit
11N/16.4

06 March 1997

LICENCE PROCEDURES TRAINING COURSE

I am writing to confirm that you have been reserved a place on the Licence
Procedures Training course to be held in training room 9/M6 in New King's
Beam House on 30 April/1st May 1997.

I am enclosing directions on how to get to NKBH, a map of the London
Underground, a list of hotels in central London (although RA6/TALU who
book training for Agency staff recommend the Strand Palace hotel which is
situated close to Charing Cross), and a Travel and Subsistence form. You
should charge all T&S claims to cost centre code 621 PPB.
Please note: You should bring your PBS Procedures manual with you to the
course.

I will be writing to you further with a timetable of events for your course nearer
the time, however, if you have any queries before then please give myself or
Kim Knight (01211 700188) a call.

Kevin Delaney

Next steps form

This is a very simple form that can be used at the end of a training course to update the trainee's personal achievement plan or as a basis for discussion with his/her manager.

ACTION PLANNING			
What action is needed?	Why is it needed?	Who should be involved?	Completion date

Course feedback form

TRAINING QUESTIONNAIRE ASSESSMENT SHEET

Previous X licensing training

1. What is your current post? ....

2. How long have you been doing this job? ....

3. How long ago did you receive Level II training? .... months.

4. Please circle the two words from the list below which together describe the Level II training you received.

  Interesting   Enjoyable   Confusing   Relevant   Dull   Boring
  Useful   Fun   Slow   Helpful   Poor   Inappropriate

5. Please use the space below if you wish to expand on your two-word description.
   ....
   ....
   ....

The remainder of the form is for assessing the effectiveness of <u>this</u> Licence Training Course

Please circle the score for each module from 5 (Very good/Very relevant) to 1 (Very poor/Irrelevant)

Joining instructions	5	4	3	2	1
DAY 1					
Spectrum management					
Module content	5	4	3	2	1
Presentation	5	4	3	2	1
Relevance to job	5	4	3	2	1
Licence process overview					
Module content	5	4	3	2	1
Presentation	5	4	3	2	1
Relevance to job	5	4	3	2	1

Admin. process

Module content	5	4	3	2	1
Presentation	5	4	3	2	1
Relevance to job	5	4	3	2	1

Technical process

Module content	5	4	3	2	1
Presentation	5	4	3	2	1
Relevance to job	5	4	3	2	1

Find the error

Module content	5	4	3	2	1
Presentation	5	4	3	2	1
Relevance to job	5	4	3	2	1

DAY 2

Cash and accounting

Module content	5	4	3	2	1
Presentation	5	4	3	2	1
Relevance to job	5	4	3	2	1

Licence entry

Module content	5	4	3	2	1
Presentation	5	4	3	2	1
Relevance to job	5	4	3	2	1

Customer care and enquiries

Module content	5	4	3	2	1
Presentation	5	4	3	2	1
Relevance to job	5	4	3	2	1

Future developments

Module content	5	4	3	2	1
Presentation	5	4	3	2	1
Relevance to job	5	4	3	2	1

Please add any comments you wish to make below:

....

....

....

....

....

Thank you.

Training evaluation form

Complete this form after the training event. The trainee and his/her manager should complete it. They may also wish to review the Next Steps Form and the Personal Achievement Plan at the same time.

TRAINING EVENT EVALUATION REPORT 1997/98

So that the Training and Agency Liaison Unit can effectively monitor training courses and therefore provide the best quality training for all RA staff, we ask you and your line manager to complete this form together and return it immediately. (If you are submitting a T&S claim, please attach this form to it).

SECTION A: COURSE MEMBER'S PERSONAL DETAILS

Title:_____Surname:_____Forenames:_____

Grade:_____Location:_____

SECTION B: COURSE DETAILS

Course Title:_____Cost:_____

Course Dates:_____ to _____

Course Objectives:_____

_____

_____

1. Were the course objectives met? (please tick)

Yes ☐ No ☐ (Please comment)_____

2. Were your own learning needs satisfied?

Yes ☐ No ☐ (Please comment)_____

3. Describe the pace of the course. (Please tick) Fast ☐ Steady ☐ Slow ☐

4. Please comment on the following. (Please tick)

Training Centre Facilities	Good ☐	Satisfactory ☐	Poor ☐
Lecture Room Facilities	Good ☐	Satisfactory ☐	Poor ☐
Course Tutor	Good ☐	Satisfactory ☐	Poor ☐
Course Literature	Good ☐	Satisfactory ☐	Poor ☐
Lunch etc Facilities (if appl)	Good ☐	Satisfactory ☐	Poor ☐

Additional Comments:_____

COURSE DETAILS CONT.

5. Could the course have been longer/shorter? (Please tick)

Yes ☐　　No ☐　　(If yes, how much longer/shorter?)_____

6. Do you think the course was value for money? (Please tick)

Yes ☐　　No ☐　　(Why?)_____

7. Would you recommend the course? (Please tick)

Yes ☐　　No ☐　　(Why?)_____

SECTION C: LINE MANAGER'S COMMENTS

1. How has this training benefitted the staff member?

2. How has this training benefitted your section/the Agency?

SECTION D: TALU'S PERFORMANCE

The Training Unit welcomes the comments you and your line manager have on their handling of this training application and subsequent enrolment.

Action aides exercise – from 75 Ways to Liven up your Training

Description   Team members assist each other in planning their next steps after the event.

Purpose   This exercise gives participants viable action planning support, and help in maintaining the team network after the event.

Materials   A flipchart and a pen for each team.
A pen for each participant.
Paper for each participant.

Duration   About 1 hour, for a team of 4.

Procedure   1. Each team member takes 5 minutes to decide on a key goal that he or she wishes to achieve during the next year. These are usually learning or business goals, but they can be personal, for example losing 25 lb (or 10 kg) of weight. The participant writes down his or her goal and name on a piece of paper.
2. The goals are then displayed for the rest of the team to see. If some of the goals are very similar they should be grouped together.
3. The team decides on the order in which the goals are going to be examined. Similar goals may be examined at the same time.
4. A member of the team writes a goal and the name of the person who owns the goal at the top of the flipchart. Below the goal, the member writes 'WHY?'. The person who owns this goal then states why he or she wishes to achieve it. Other members of the team may ask for clarification and discuss the reasoning. The reason is then written on the flipchart.
5. Next, 'WHEN' is written, and agreement is reached on when the goal is to be achieved.
6. 'HOW' is then written on the flipchart. This is the difficult question. The team helps the goal owner to draw up an action plan, or list the steps required to achieve the goal. Remember that 'by the inch it's a cinch, by the yard it's hard'. When the necessary steps have been determined, the team decides which of its members can help the goal owner to take each step. Against each step, 'WHO' is written, together with the name of the person who will help and when the step will be achieved. It may be necessary to review the end date for the plan in the light of the intermediate steps. Once the plan has been agreed, it is signed by all the team members.
7. The team then moves on to the next goal. If there are a number of similar action plans, these should be considered at the same time.
8. The process continues until all the members of the team have action plans.

Review   None.

Variations   None.

RECOMMENDED READING

The books/articles listed below are those which I have found helpful since I became involved in people development. Some are general management or organizational behaviour books, whilst others are more concerned with learning and training. The title is a good indication of the type of book. I hope you will also find them helpful.

Bee, F. and R., *Training Needs Analysis and Evaluation*, IPD, 1994.

Belasco, J., *Teaching the Elephant to Dance*, Century Business, 1991.

Block, P., *Flawless Consulting – A Guide to Getting Your Expertise Used*, Learning Concepts, 1978.

Cockman, P., Evans, B. and Reynolds, P., *Client-Centred Consulting*, McGraw-Hill, 1992.

Crawley, J., *Constructive Conflict Management*, Nicholas Brealey, 1995.

Handscome, R. and Norman, P., *Strategic Leadership*, McGraw-Hill, 1993.

Jaques, D., *Learning in Groups*, Kogan Page, 1991.

Kolb, D., *Experiential Learning*, Prentice Hall, 1984.

Luft, J., *Group Processes – An Introduction to Group Dynamics*, Mayfield Publishing Co., 1970.

Morgan, G., *Images of Organisation*, Sage, 1994.

Orridge, M., *75 Ways to Liven Up Your Training*, Gower, 1996.

Reid, M. and Barrington, H., *Training Interventions – Managing People Development*, IPD, 1994.

Savage, C., *5th Generation Management*, Digital Press, 1990.

Senge, P., *The Fifth Discipline*, Doubleday, 1992.

Tuckman, B., and Jenson, M., *Stages of Small Group Development*, Group & Organisational Studies, 1977.

Tyson, S. and York, A., *Personnel Management*, Butterworth-Heinemann, 1993.

Waterman, R., *The Renewal Factor*, Bantam Press, 1988.

INDEX